THE DESIGN MIX

WILEY

CONTENTS

KABARET'S PROPHECY, LONDON, 2004, DESIGNED BY DAVID COLLINS WITH ILLUSTRATIONS BY JAMIE HEWLETT, CREATOR OF TANK GIRL & PART OF THE BAND GORILLAZ.

PREFACE

This book celebrates the fantastic renaissance of both bar design and cocktail culture in recent years. More bars are better designed than ever, and the cocktails they serve share in a quest for innovation, adventure and quality. When a new bar really hits the mark, the designer's interesting use of materials, colours, textures and effects is matched by the mixologist's own sense of design. In the very best bars and restaurants, the mixologist has often explored a variety of ingredients to create a refreshing blend of interesting flavours that emphasise the uniqueness of the bar and form an integral part of the 'design mix'.

As far as cocktails are concerned, my mixology philosophy is simple: by respecting and understanding your ingredients you can learn how to combine them to achieve the most important thing in a cocktail – the balance of flavours. I always use only the very best ingredients. If possible I emphasise seasonal and regional produce, the freshest juices and best mixers, liquors etc. Also, it's best not to use too many ingredients: you want to complement, rather than mask, a quality spirit's subtle flavour. A yardstick for this is no more than five or six ingredients within the cocktail.

Mixology and bar culture are at the most exciting time in their history. The world's best mixologists – some of whom have contributed to this book – now have an incredible depth of knowledge and are fast becoming as respected as top class chefs. Collaborating with Bombay Sapphire for the last couple of years, I have been driving concepts such as pairing food with cocktails, working

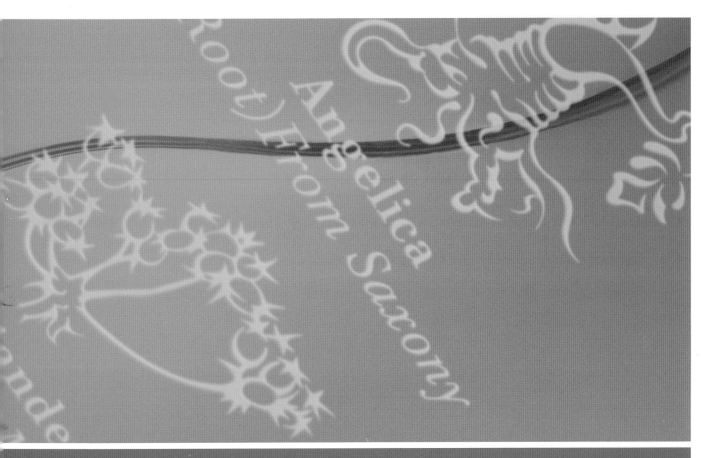

alongside top chefs at award-winning restaurants around the world. On the downside; sometimes all this excitement can cause a few problems with bartenders running before they can walk, i.e. too many ingredients or certain ingredients added to the drink just for the sake of being extravagant (squid ink martini cocktail anyone?!).

I believe we should have a huge amount of respect for the classic cocktails of the past but, then again, if we embrace the belief that all the best cocktails have already been made the world of cocktail-making would be a rather dull place.

My angle is to capture and understand all the ingredients that contribute to making a great cocktail into a classic one and to use this knowledge to create exciting new drinks. For **The Design Mix – Bars, Cocktails & Style**, I have created a range of new cocktails inspired by the wonderful bars and restaurants included in the book, drawing on local culture and regional flavours as well as the designs and specialities of the establishments themselves. They could be the classics of tomorrow.

JAMIE WALKER
MIXOLOGIST

INTRODUCTION

The onyx glow of the bar counter; the luxuriously soft leather of the armchair that coaxes us to relax and appreciate the DJ's fresh, slightly heady mix; the anticipation of the taste of the mixologist's new cocktail; the simple grace of the Martini glass ... More than ever, we are aware that design is everywhere and can play an essential part in answering the desire for adventure, pleasure and luxury. People are searching to push the boundaries of their experience through fashion, travel, tastes and textures. Our ideas of luxury and style have been substantially changed and cocktail culture has met the clarion call for uniqueness. Bars have become the vortex for innovative design, with fresh, inspirational interiors matched by a peerless era for cocktails.

The world's leading designers are queuing up to confound expectations of bar design, while the likes of Karim Rashid, Marcel Wanders and Marc Newson have also turned their attention to reinventing cocktail shakers and glassware. Meanwhile, mixologists have become international superstars, winning admirers through their own take on design: how flavours can be combined and balanced for new sensations. The customers are more design literate than ever; they are discerning, open-minded and individualistic, and this has given designers a new freedom to integrate a myriad of influences to create newly adventurous micro-worlds. *The Design Mix* is a celebration of bars and cocktails from across the world, and is infused with the variety of cultural deviations that make cocktail drinking so endlessly interesting and entertaining.

The range and quality of bars is a new phenomenon, but bars and cocktails have long been a signifier of design and architectural trends, while also interacting with film, music, literature, fashion and art. The speed with which cocktail culture can absorb and adapt different influences makes it a natural hub for new styles and flavours. It's no surprise that beautiful, adventurous new bars draw fashionistas like moths to a flame. However, beyond acting as a barometer for sometimes flighty trends, the design mix that makes up cocktail culture is highly sophisticated and alters our relationship with the built environment. As a public arena for cultural life, the bar world's response to minimalism has had a long-term effect on the way we understand luxury, beyond gilded ostentation. Bars have been instrumental in introducing the aesthetic of simplicity and grace. After all, one of the original masterpieces of modernism is Vienna's Kärntner Bar, Adolph Loos' 1908 design which rejected the elaborate ornamentation of Art Nouveau.

Historically, it is easy to associate cocktail culture with class. We think of the old idea of the cocktail hour as a society thing, perhaps involving upper-class English girls breaking off from croquet to get a little squiffy while trying to think of witty things to say. One of the joys of the new era is that cocktails still carry the air of quality, but with a different demographic – they are an expression of knowledge, taste, pleasure and individuality, and not of the rights of birth. This has allowed cocktail culture to blossom in the modern age. Their appeal is wider than ever, but their sophistication has not been debased by popularity. In truth, our idea of cocktail society has always been skewed. After all, most cocktails actually have their origins in medicinal concoctions for sailors or a classless American passion for hard liquor.

Cocktail culture is completely rife with highly imaginative, romantic and often apocryphal stories, especially concerning the origins of the classic cocktails. One thing that can be verified is that the first recorded use of the word 'cocktail' was in an American publication called *The Balance* in 1806 ('… cocktail is a stimulating liquor, composed of spirits of any kind, sugar, water, and bitters'), but the idea of flavouring or mixing drinks – largely for medicinal purposes – predates this by several centuries. Cordials distilled with juniper were already widely drunk in Europe by the 14th century in the belief that they would protect from the plague. Alcohol became recognised as a pleasant medium for imbibing medicinal ingredients as well as acting as a preservative. The regular, pre-meal ingestion of infused distilled drinks, usually based on wine, became indoctrinated into social ritual and known as the aperitif. Meanwhile, in the 19th

century, an American passion for sweet, spirit-based drinks had become rampant. The merging of the ideas of the European, high-class, pre-dinner aperitif and American, spirit-based concoctions happened towards the end of the 19th century, led by wealthy Americans conducting cultural tours of Europe. European hotels began to cater for the taste for these spirit-based cocktails, which were known as 'American drinks', and consequently opened 'American bars', some of which are still in existence to this day.

Modern cocktails really made their mark in Britain with the opening of the bar at Claridge's in 1899, and cocktails started to replace the aperitif as a high-society, pre-dinner tipple. According to the *Sphere* newspaper at that time, Claridge's barmaid Ada Coleman was the first woman to mix and serve cocktails in Britain, starting off with a Manhattan. She moved to the Savoy's American Bar in 1903 where she continued to serve cocktails until 1924, bowing out with a Martini for the Prince of Wales. By then, the upper echelons really had got the cocktail bug. Drinking cocktails in fine bars had become the height of fashion and went hand in hand with a slightly risqué love of pleasure, luxury and new experiences.

The relationship between cocktails, class and style was emphasised during Prohibition. In the early 20th century, New York in particular was abuzz with a sense of freedom, with revolutionary skyscrapers announcing the unbridled self-assurance, optimism and ambition of the city. It was a party town, moving at a rate that is unimaginable in European cities. The party was supposed to be punctured on 16 January 1920 with the National Prohibition Act which forebade the manufacture, sale or transportation of intoxicating liquor. Ironically, Prohibition made cocktails even more popular. In a new culture of wild private parties and speakeasies, cocktails helped disguise the taste of poor quality, homemade and bootlegged alcohol. There was a new reverence for well-crafted, quality imported spirits and the reputation of London gin and Scotch whisky was greatly enhanced. New cocktail recipes, many of which became the classics of today, thrived and were often engraved into cocktail accessories such as shakers, glasses and measures. At this time, cocktail culture became caught up with

innovative design. On both sides of the Atlantic, cocktail style became firmly aligned to Art Deco, an association which continues to this day. Art Deco was cool, streamlined and innovative – it suggested that the fuss and ephemera of the previous century were firmly in the past and was associated with looking forward into a fast, modern Machine Age. Cocktails and skyscrapers reflected what New Yorkers thought about themselves: stylish, innovative and decadent. The classic cocktail receptacle had been based on the old English teapot (because refined English ladies had taken to discreetly serving gin at tea parties!), but now it took on the sleek lines and chrome of Art Deco and many were designed as mini-skyscrapers. Meanwhile, Art Deco-designed cocktail bars, such as the Savoy's American Bar with its 1930s redesign, were the most sophisticated, stylish and adventurous places to be seen, with their radical design matched by the potent new drinks.

Cocktail culture became so ingrained in people's idea of class, sophistication and style that it was increasingly used in music, literature and films to suggest mood and identify character traits. The works of F Scott Fitzgerald, Ernest Hemingway and Raymond Chandler are infused with references to particular drinks. Part of the popularity of the Daiquiri, the Gimlet and the Mojito is down to these writers. Cocktails were also associated with the dry, worldly and irreverent wit of the Algonquin Round Table and Dorothy Parker, who famously wrote, 'I wish I could drink like a lady. I can take one or two at the most. Three and I'm under the table. Four and I'm under the host.' The songs of Noel Coward, Cole Porter and Ivor Novello are also caught up in the wit of the cocktail age. Of course, cocktails have had a long association with the glitz of Hollywood and the film world, often used in films to display quality, class and sophistication. James Bond is perhaps the most famous example of a character whose

attitude is exemplified by his relation to a cocktail, usually a Vodka Martini: 'shaken not stirred'. Held in the hands of Greta Garbo, Frank Sinatra, Humphrey Bogart, Joan Crawford or Bette Davis, particular drinks highlighted character traits in a myriad of ways. *The Thin Man* is one of the greatest cocktail movies – the high-class, gentleman detective Nick is portrayed as sharp, dry and suave, ever ready with a killer line. Consequently, he is never far away from his next Martini. With the return of the

cocktail to its former heights, the connection is back, particularly in films such as *Swingers* and the Coen Brothers' *The Big Lebowski*.

The Wall Street Crash, the Great Depression and the Second World War literally took the fizz out of cocktail society. Long after the end of the war, rationing, 'making do' and a far-reaching austerity ensured that the optimism and glamour that accompany the popularity of

THERE WAS A GREAT SHIFT TOWARDS INNOVATIVE BAR DESIGNS IN EUROPE IN THE MID-1990S WITH THE LIKES OF CAFÉ L'ATLANTIQUE, DESIGNED BY FABIO NOVEMBRE, IN MILAN.

bar and cocktail culture were very far from the forefront of people's minds. For better or worse, the rise of Tiki culture in the 1950s and 1960s was to put the fun back into cocktails, but the real downturn in cocktail style was in the 1980s, when a new genre of pink-neon cocktail bars surfaced to meet the needs of the wealthy, shoulder-padded 'Me Generation'. This association with superficial, flashy wealth rather than sophisticated style was damaging to the reputation of cocktails, but fortunately the pink neon all but flickered its last some time ago. In the 1990s, the real heart of cocktail culture was reborn.

With a new breed of sophisticated, stylish, curious and discerning drinkers demanding more than bland, mass-produced drinks in identikit pubs and bars, hotel bars, members clubs and cocktail bars have been reborn as beautifully designed, unique havens. Particularly in Britain, chains have taken over many high-street bars and pubs, making them all look the same. The world's leading designers have created the antidote, with a new, passionate approach to materials, form and luxury that is inspiring, sophisticated and radical. More than ever, the psychology of design has been understood and acted upon, offering us a sense of individuality, exclusivity and adventure through bespoke creations. Yet these bars are nothing without their mixologists, who ensure that the classic cocktails are perfect while also twisting them into unique variations, applying a science of balance and taste that has opened up previously unchart waters. In a time when we are so often made weary by our knowledge and worldliness, these bars take us on an adventure of the senses. Long may this new golden age continue.

Roppongi Hills Club is serious business in that it's the prime gathering point for the financial and cultural elite of Tokyo, but it's also seriously pleasurable. It's a members' club of extraordinarily high ideals that, as its own message states, 'functions as a forum where global thought and sensibilities abound, a place with the ability to inspire lively conversations that transcend the limitations of one's work or generation'. Fortunately, the setting for these noble intentions is a magnificent array of bars and restaurants where the emphasis is on high quality aesthetics and cuisine.

The club is situated on the 51st floor of the Roppongi Hills Mori Tower, an office and arts building that is the centrepiece of the redevelopment of the Roppongi area of Tokyo as a cultural district. The tower and, in fact, much of the new Roppongi, has been created by Minoru Mori, one of Japan's most famous businessmen whose investments in urban regeneration continually defy any thoughts that Japan will never recover from the bursting of the bubble economy. The club makes full use of the views over Tokyo. One of Britain's leading designers, Sir Terence Conran, has designed the interior so that there is a virtually unbroken 360-degree view of the city – this marries with the club's philosophy: its members may be the financial elite (the numbing initial joining fee is almost $10,000) but Mori wishes them to be outward-looking, reflecting on the state of the world while sipping their fine cocktails.

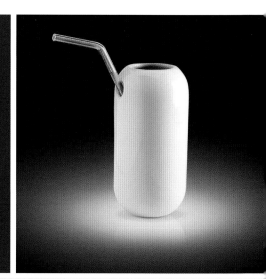

EQUIPPED WITH STYLE: CANNETTE WITH STRAW

EVERY PRODUCT AVAILABLE AT THE CONRAN SHOP IS SAID TO BE PASSED PERSONALLY BY SIR TERENCE CONRAN. THE TUBULAR, CERAMIC CANETTE, WHICH FEATURES A GLASS STRAW, IS A HIGHLY UNUSUAL COCKTAIL RECEPTACLE, AVAILABLE FROM WWW.CONRAN.COM.

THE DESIGNER:
SIR TERENCE CONRAN

BORN IN 1931, SIR TERENCE CONRAN ESTABLISHED THE FIRST HABITAT, THE CHAIN OFTEN HERALDED AS STARTING THE DEMOCRATISATION OF GOOD DESIGN & REVOLUTIONISING BRITISH HOME INTERIORS, IN 1964. HE WENT ON TO SET UP THE CONRAN SHOP & THE BENCHMARK WOODWORK COMPANY, & HAS LAUNCHED MANY RESTAURANTS INCLUDING QUAGLINO'S, BLUEBIRD & FLORIDITA, A NEW CUBAN-INFLUENCED RESTAURANT IN LONDON. HE WAS BEHIND THE INITIATION OF LONDON'S DESIGN MUSEUM IN 1989, WHILE CONRAN & PARTNERS' OWN DESIGNS INCLUDE THE GREAT EASTERN HOTEL IN LONDON & THE PARK HOTEL, BANGALORE. AS WELL AS THE ROPPONGI HILLS CLUB, JAPANESE VENTURES INCLUDE THE ARK HILLS CLUB WHICH HOUSES PAINTINGS BY LE CORBUSIER.

All the club's facilities are set on the outer perimeter of the building, which is oval with the exception of two bulbous, cornea-like protrusions on opposite sides. These house two of the club's larger facilities, the Fifty One Club and the Meridiana restaurant. The Fifty One Club, an informal brasserie and bar, is simply designed with white tablecloths and Mart Stam's black cantilever chairs, but has full floor-to-ceiling glazing to make the most of the views of Tokyo Bay. The Meridiana is an Italian restaurant, bar and lounge with an orange theme that begins with the neon floorstrip and curving wall of the reception and is picked up by the furniture, including Bombo bar stools. The bar specialises in organic juices that 'women will appreciate'!

Both liquor and more innovative design come into their own with the more intimate Sushi Bar, a sleek, black-lacquer box with an alluring, colourful flower mural and mirrored saké display. The Star Bar, the similarly simple but effective cocktail bar, features Pierre Paulin's Slice chairs, pointing upwards towards the star-dotted ceiling which continues the night-sky view of central Tokyo. The Star Bar has a regular Scotch night, but Martini drinkers should head to the bar and lounge of the Undercurrent restaurant, which serves 21 varieties. Elsewhere, Conran has really delved into Japanese design with Onjaku, a Kappo cuisine restaurant with dishes designed to complement saké. The sublime spaces feature floor seats with graceful, arching back supports, a tearoom with purple tatami mats, a falling-water sculpture and modern Japanese screens. Other restaurants include the Star Anise, specialising in Chinese (rather than Japanese) saké and teas. Its all-red private booths are the most full-on sensual rooms in the whole club design.

ROPPONGI HILLS CLUB, TOKYO

ROPPONGI HILLS CLUB
ROPPONGI HILLS MORI TOWER,
6-10-1 ROPPONGI, MINATO-KU,
TOKYO 106-6151, JAPAN

TEL +81 (0)3 6406 6001
WWW.ROPPONGIHILLSCLUB.COM

INSPIRED CREATIONS:
SAKE BOMB MARTINI BY JAMIE WALKER

INSPIRED BY THE QUALITIES OF SAKÉ & ITS VARIETY OF FLAVOURS, JAMIE WALKER HAS CREATED A NEW COCKTAIL WHICH BALANCES A RHUBARB VERSION OF JAPAN'S NATIONAL DRINK WITH THE DRY PROPERTIES OF GIN & CRANBERRY.

INGREDIENTS:
35 ML (1 OZ) BOMBAY SAPPHIRE GIN
10 ML (0.3 OZ) RHUBARB SAKÉ
50 ML (1.5 OZ) CRANBERRY JUICE
SQUEEZE OF FRESH LIME

METHOD:
SHAKE WITH ICE & STRAIN
GLASS: MARTINI
GARNISH: NONE

Almost all the restaurants have private dining rooms, specifically created to impress business clients, while the Amakawa *tepanyaki* restaurant is entirely private. Guests sit at a table arcing around the personal chef's station while taking in the view of Tokyo Bay. Throughout the Roppongi Hills Club, the design and facilities are a physical embodiment of the co-relationship of work and play. Private club culture first emerged in Regency London, primarily out of a need to create protected enclaves for gambling and business, but there is a continued British embarrassment about the connection between work and pleasure. By contrast, the Japanese have no coyness about merging the two, and Roppongi Hills Club is a conscious temple to the benefits of their symbiosis. It is simultaneously strange and fitting, then, that the designer is British.

TMSK, the leading Shanghai bar and restaurant, is inspired by a high-design concept that has been beautifully and fluently realised. TMSK is the acronym for Tou Ming Si Kao, which can be roughly translated as 'crystal mind' or 'transparent thinking'; the design is informed by the transparency and beauty of glass along with a quest for artistic purity. The result is not just the best restaurant design in Shanghai; the cohesion of the design, extending from the interior to the food and the music, makes this one of the best-executed restaurant concepts in the world. In recent years, the economic climate change in China has prepared the way for Shanghai – always such a fascinating, cutting-edge, bustling and unique city, benefiting from its position at a crossroads of influences – to return to its place as one of the great cultural centres. The glinting jewel of TMSK ensures that there is still a Shanghai surprise for even the most world-weary traveller.

TMSK is a spin-off from Liuli Gongfang, the glass design company which is now establishing a worldwide reputation. *Liuli* is an archaic Chinese word for glass. As co-owner Chang Yi told the *Taipei Times*, liuli was chosen over the commonly used word *boli* because, 'Everyone knows what glass is, and when you hear it you immediately think of a material, like bottles, glasses. *Liuli* is more refined and embodies Chinese culture and history.' The word holds within it the idea of traditional craftsmanship. Chang, a former film director, set up Liuli Gongfang with partner and actress Loretta Yang Hui-shan when they surprised everybody by walking away from the film industry in 1987. Their designs have made them famous all over again and they have become the unofficial

ambassadors for the art of *liuli*. TMSK, which opened in 2001, puts the art form into a social context. *Liuli* is used throughout the design, from furniture and table settings to floors and a particularly impressive vaulted ceiling of glass discs in the main dining hall. Many of the elements are inspired by the beauty of nature.

The best place for cocktails is the Orchid Pond lounge, which features a raised, rectangular pool of water decorated with rows of *liuli* orchid blossoms, each sitting in its own circle of coloured light coming from below. Stately, gold-and-red-covered chairs sit on patterned metal flooring but the effect is not gaudy. The room is deliberately dark and moody; as the owners say, 'Light must be toned down. With this the eye pupils will dilate, and see more, and more distinctly, the rich variety of the shades of intricate details.' Detail is the key to TMSK's success – every element is crafted and its effect is considered as part of the whole, while lighting is carefully engineered throughout to allow the brilliance of individual designs to be picked out without being lost in a garish gleam. The bar counter itself is a work of art. The front is made entirely of glass, with green circles

THE DESIGNER: LUILI GONGFANG

TMSK, WHICH RANKS HIGH AMONGST THE BEST-DESIGNED RESTAURANTS & BARS IN THE WORLD, IS THE CREATION OF THE GLASS COMPANY LIULI GONGFANG, WHICH HAS REINVIGORATED THE ANCIENT CHINESE ART OF GLASSMAKING. IT NOW HAS OVER 50 STORES WORLDWIDE, SELLING EVERYTHING FROM HANDCRAFTED TABLEWARE TO JEWELLERY TO SCULPTURE. LORETTA YANG HUI-SHAN, WHO CO-FOUNDED THE COMPANY WITH CHANG YI, WAS A FAMOUS ACTRESS BEFORE SHE GAVE UP ACTING TO FOCUS ON GLASS DESIGN. ALMOST EVERY ELEMENT OF TMSK IS HAND-CRAFTED, FROM THE VAULTED GLASS CEILING TO THE COLOURED GLASSWARE. THE DESIGNERS SAY THAT TMSK WAS INSPIRED BY THE TANG DYNASTY: 'FIRST WE PICTURE A SCENE OF EXTRAVAGANT LUXURY TYPICAL OF THE LATER TANG DYNASTY, A SCENE OF RESPLENDENT BEAUTY. THEN IN OUR IMAGINATION WE LIGHT UP THE LAMPS & LANTERNS OF OVER 1,000 YEARS AGO, & THEN WE LET ALL THE DECORATIVE DETAILS SOMEHOW FADE OUT & RECEDE INTO A PREGNANT HALF-LIGHT.'

EQUIPPED WITH STYLE: MARTINI GLASS BY MARTIN WANDERS

LORETTA YANG HUI-SHAN, THE DESIGNER OF TMSK BAR & RESTAURANT IN SHANGHAI, HAS BEEN A JUDGE IN THE ANNUAL BOMBAY SAPPHIRE DESIGNER GLASS COMPETITION WHICH SETS OUT TO REWARD INNOVATION IN GLASSWARE DESIGN. THE 2005 JUDGES ALSO INCLUDED WELL-KNOWN MOULD-BREAKERS SUCH AS TOM DIXON & MARCEL WANDERS, THE DUTCH DESIGNER WHO FIRST MADE HIS NAME WITH THE DROOG COLLECTIVE. WANDERS IS FAMOUS FOR HIS UNUSUAL & OFTEN HUMOROUS APPROACH TO THE DESIGN OF EVERYDAY OBJECTS. PICTURED LEFT IS HIS TAKE ON THE CLASSIC MARTINI GLASS.

TMSK, SHANGHAI

TMSK
UNIT 2, NO 11 BEILI,
XINTIANDI SQUARE, LANE 181,
TAICONG ROAD, SHANGHAI, CHINA

TEL +86 (0)21 63262227
WWW.TMSK.COM

INSPIRED CREATIONS: SAPPHIRE TANG MARTINI

MIXOLOGIST JAMIE WALKER PICKS UP ON TMSK'S TANG DESIGN INFLUENCE & THE CLASSIC CHINESE FLAVOURS OF LYCHEE & GREEN TEA TO CREATE A NEW MARTINI COCKTAIL.

INGREDIENTS:
35 ML (1 OZ) BOMBAY SAPPHIRE GIN
5 ML (0.15 OZ) LYCHEE LIQUEUR
10 ML (0.3 OZ) GREEN TEA LIQUEUR
10 ML (0.3 OZ) FRESH LYCHEE JUICE
SQUEEZE OF FRESH LIME

METHOD:
SHAKE WITH ICE & STRAIN
GLASS: MARTINI
GARNISH: SKEWERED LYCHEE

standing upon a range of coloured squares. The bar stools are round seats placed on the top of fuchsia-coloured glass vases, helping to create a crystal kaleidoscope. Familiar lantern designs are reinterpreted throughout the restaurant, VIP and bar areas, while other traditional elements include red and black lacquered tables and typically Chinese chairs in the bar. Liuli Gongfang craftsmanship extends to the sculptural tableware and the range of interestingly shaped glasses with different-coloured stems.

The design addresses itself as a 'throwback to Tang dynasty China', but the interpretation is extremely modern. It draws on the refinement of the past but contextualises

it with modern references and translates its beauty as a refreshing, inimitable experience for a new audience. And TMSK is an experience. The upstairs dining area includes the Little Stage where *pingtan* opera is performed, but the traditional instruments of the *san-xian* (three-stringed banjo) and the *pipa* (four-stringed lute) are blended with electronic beats to create a new mix. Like the design, the French-influenced food is imbued with a sense of balance, delicacy and coloured translucency. The signature Liuli Pâté, for instance, is a cross-section of fresh vegetables and French pâté set into a glass-like, translucent orange gel. The international wine list is approaching 300 choices, while the emphasis on precise artistry extends to the cocktails.

SKETCH

Opening a £10-million, high-design emporium of restaurant, bar and gallery spaces in the former headquarters of both the Royal Institute of British Architects and Christian Dior, king of the revolutionary 'New Look', is nothing if not brave. However, even though it opened back in 2002, there's still a real buzz about Sketch, kept alive not by the surfeit of celebrity customers, but by a uniqueness that has survived both criticism and fads. Its success lies in its desire to offer an increasingly design-literate public living, responsive, interactive spaces that really engage while confounding expectations and delighting the senses. Sketch is an evolving work, with the Glade restaurant and the redesigned Parlour, completed in late 2005, the most significant new ventures.

The Grade II-listed 1779 town house on London's Conduit Street is now home to a chic, extravagant melange where the design, food and cocktails combine to offer a fresh frisson. Owner Mourad Mazouz had already found success in London with the very sensual Maghrebi restaurant Momo, and here teamed up with co-owner and chef Pierre Gagnaire, architect Gabhan O'Keeffe and interior designer Noé Duchaufour-Lawrance to create a series of rooms that continue to have even design-spoilt, world-weary Londoners slipping on their most stylish togs. Specially commissioned pieces from some of the world's leading designers, including Ron Arad, Marc Newson and Jurgen Bey, add to the surprise factor and help blur the distinction between gallery and entertainment spaces.

In the entranceway, Ron Arad's one-piece, sculptural chair-desk and Jurgen Bey's grand chairs, morphing out of a wall of elasticised skin, announce that Sketch wears its nonconformity on its sleeve. The stairs drip with different shades of chocolate resin, suggesting the decadence that lies within, but in the end it is the bars and restaurants that have to deliver rather than these introductory showpieces. Fortunately, they do just that. The principal bars are the East Bar and, just by the entrance, the Parlour, which was originally more of a patisserie but has been redesigned by Mazouz to suit its additional night-time lounge activity. The space is awash with 60 different fabrics and manages to combine elements of a rustic French farmhouse, a contemporary-design lover's living room and touches of Versailles opulence. Wall-mounted animal heads, velvet wall coverings and luxuriant daybeds rival the strong graphic patterns of the 1960s-style curtains, white kitchen cupboards and wooden chairs with backs shaped as an 'O'. Patisserie fare is still available but the Parlour now has an all-day licence and is a fittingly relaxed place for a cocktail.

THE MIXOLOGIST: TONY GEARY

TONY GEARY OF SKETCH (FORMERLY OF EAST@WEST IN LONDON & ANGUS IN SYDNEY) SAYS, 'A GOOD BAR IS THE RIGHT BALANCE OF MANY FACTORS: GREAT PEOPLE WHO KNOW HOW TO ENJOY THEMSELVES – CUSTOMERS & STAFF ALIKE; INSPIRED DRINKS THAT APPEAL TO ALL; MUSIC TO SET THE SCENE; WITH BEAUTIFUL, COMFORTABLE & CLEAN SURROUNDINGS.' ONE OF SKETCH'S SIGNATURE DRINKS IS THE BUTTERFLY CATCHER, A LONG SUMMER DRINK BALANCING THE SWEETNESS OF BLACKBERRY BRANDY (CRÈME DE MURE), THE SHARPNESS OF PINK GRAPEFRUIT & THE DRYNESS OF GIN.

BUTTERFLY CATCHER
INGREDIENTS:
50 ML (1.5 OZ) BOMBAY SAPPHIRE GIN
25 ML (0.75 OZ) ELDERFLOWER CORDIAL
50 ML (1.5 OZ) PINK GRAPEFRUIT
10 ML (0.3 OZ) CRÈME DE MURE

METHOD:
SHAKE ALL INGREDIENTS EXCEPT THE CRÈME DE MURE, STRAIN OVER CRUSHED ICE INTO A GLASS, & FLOAT THE MURE ON TOP
GLASS: COLLINS
GARNISH: LEMON TWIST

The ovoid East Bar, or at least its lavoratory cubicles, is probably the most photographed aspect of Sketch. From the outside, the bar is a large white egg surrounded on either side by staircases leading to 12 individual, enclosed, pod-like toilets. The bar itself, lit with pink neon, is very space age and ambient, with inflatable seating around the wall and a pink, circular counter in the centre. The former West Bar has given way to the daytime Glade Restaurant which, as the name suggests, has been designed as a forest glade. The sprawling, entwining braches of the central chandelier hang over chunky wooden tables and green carpeting. Pierre Gagnaire's menu received stunning reviews as soon as the restaurant opened and the Glade provides a less expensive alternative to the Lecture Room and Library. When Sketch first opened, it was the prices in these, as well as the design, that had some critics slack-jawed. Nowadays, the prices no longer seem so out of the ordinary, but the design and atmosphere remain unique. Created by Gabhan O'Keeffe, the rooms are a citric twist on old-fashioned expectations of opulence. Sunbursts, studded leather walls,

SKETCH, LONDON

SKETCH
9 CONDUIT STREET,
LONDON
W1S 2XG, UK

TEL +44 (0)870 777 4488
WWW.SKETCH.UK.COM

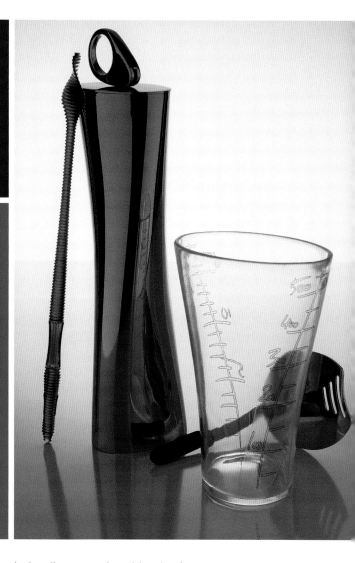

EQUIPPED WITH STYLE:
THE CHIRINGUITO COCKTAIL SHAKER AND TWISTER BY RON ARAD AND ALBERTO GOZZI

THE SHAFT OF THE POLISHED STAINLESS-STEEL SHAKER (CREATED IN 2004 FOR WWW.ALESSI.COM) IS TWISTED TO SUGGEST THE MOTION OF THE LIQUID INSIDE. AS WELL AS CONTRIBUTING TO THE DESIGN OF SKETCH, RON ARAD IS FAMOUS FOR HIS FURNITURE DESIGNS, INCLUDING THE TOM VAC CHAIR, & RECENTLY DESIGNED A FLOOR OF THE HOTEL PUERTA AMÉRICA, MADRID.

stuffed velvet chairs and oversized urns create a quietly disconcerting blend of traditionalism and exoticism, which is mirrored by the impressive tasting menus.

Sketch is an all-day event, with the Parlour opening for breakfast and the Gallery providing a free, public art space. Beneath a large, circular skylight, the latter has low leatherette-covered banquettes for customers to watch video art on conjoined screens. At night, the Gallery is transformed into a relaxed brasserie, with the banquettes replaced by white dining chairs and figure-of-eight tables on highly decorated supports. It stays open until the early hours for music, cocktails and video projections.

FRISSON

Attaining a certain frisson is supposed to be an accident of chemistry rather than an achievable scientific quest: there are plenty of restaurants that have good design or good food but fail to create any electric charge amongst the customers and can consequently feel dead as a dodo. You can hire the right chef, the right designer, the right mixologist and sommelier, spending a fortune along the way, but dinner guests can end up sitting there in a joyless vacuum, even though they might appreciate the various individual components. By calling itself Frisson, this new San Franciscan restaurant and bar could have been asking for trouble, but somewhere along the line, the team behind it have secured the magic formula: the atmosphere fizzes with possibilities.

It helps when you get all the principal elements right. Frisson, which opened in 2004, started life with acclaimed chef Daniel Patterson – famous for his obsession with aromas and working with a parfumier to design dishes – and now has Sarah Schafer, who has added her own touch of originality to the 'New American' menu, at the helm. Meanwhile, Duggan McDonnell, Frisson's award-winning 'bar chef', has created an innovative cocktail menu inspired by California's rich variety of fresh produce. 'New classics' include his Renaissance Negroni, with sweet vermouth replaced by Liqueur de Poete, a specialist pear brandy liqueur created locally in the Bay Area.

The good food and drink help make the atmosphere, but the design has played a huge part in setting the social tone at Frisson. In the last few years

CLASSIC COCKTAILS
THE NEGRONI

ONE OF FRISSON'S SIGNATURE COCKTAILS IS THE RENAISSANCE NEGRONI, A DRIER VERSION OF A CLASSIC NEGRONI WHICH IN TURN IS BASED ON THE AMERICANO, A MARTINI & SWEET VERMOUTH MIX WHICH WAS VERY POPULAR, PARTICULARLY IN ITALY IN THE 1920S. THE NEGRONI WAS APPARENTLY INVENTED AT THE JACOSA BAR IN FLORENCE WHEN COUNT CAMILLO NEGRONI ASKED FOR HIS AMERICANO TO BE GIVEN A STRONGER EDGE WITH THE HELP OF A SHOT OF GIN.

INGREDIENTS:
30 ML (1 OZ) GIN
30 ML (1 OZ) MARTINI EXTRA DRY VERMOUTH
30 ML (1 OZ) BITTERS

METHOD:
BUILD INTO A ROCKS GLASS FILLED WITH ICE & STIR
GLASS: OLD-FASHIONED
GARNISH: SLICE OF ORANGE

both Fabio Novembre and Karim Rashid, two of the world's leading designers, have explored the means of creating a dynamic social atmosphere in bars and restaurants through furniture design. At the restaurant of Novembre's Una Hotel Vittoria in Florence, all the diners sit at the same S-shaped table, which means that each individual is seated opposite several others, potentially from other groups. Rashid, meanwhile, has developed his curving Omni sofas which can be linked to form amorphous circles or wiggles that bring out the possibilities of social interplay. At Frisson, the designer Scott Kester and Architecture TM have created a rotunda, which immediately has the effect of collectively embracing all the individuals groups held within. Kester is inspired by the golden age of Art Deco cruise ships where life was structured around sociable ballroom dances and dinner events in luxurious surroundings. At Frisson, all the details encourage the sense that although people might be strangers, this is a shared experience. Within the main room, which is centred on a circular dome decorated with aureoles of illuminated perforations, the sight lines are completely without interruption.

The walls of the rotunda are formed by an outer circle of banquettes and three screens of semitranslucent, overlapping resin panels which create an interesting, fractured texture and offer a colour contrast to the warm orange and browns of the furnishings. The principal seating is made up of wool-covered, semicircular banquettes with mahogany backs, designed by Kester. In the middle, all the banquettes are connected to a central hub, so they are like tentacles reaching out into the room from the same mass – very inclusive, very sociable. They are accompanied by Visitor chairs designed by Eero Saarinen and walnut tables, thereby merging contemporary innovation, 20th-century classic design and the materials of traditional luxury in one fell swoop. Frisson has a connected bar area, featuring hexagonal ottomans designed by Kester and dominated by an artwork by Catherine Wagner set above the bottle display. Called *Flux Density*, it is a 24-foot photographic mural of

FRISSON, SAN FRANCISCO

FRISSON
244 JACKSON STREET,
SAN FRANCISCO,
CA 94111, USA

TEL +1 415 956 3004
WWW.FRISSONSF.COM

champagne bubbles. The bar has its own cocktail-life, but interaction with the main dining space is continuous, with moments glimpsed through the spaces in the resin-panel screens. The bar lives on after the restaurant stops serving, with the banquettes of the main dining space helping smooth its transition into a lounge. Elsewhere, as has become customary in fine restaurants, there is a chef's table, here set in a private room which opens onto the kitchen. An intimate, sultry mood is created by brown leather and dark tweed, but a shaggy, coconut light provides a touch of humour. The restrooms are unisex, adding another touch of frisson.

Koji Imai and Foodscope's Megu restaurant and Kimono bar, housed in a 19th-century, cast-iron framed building in Tribeca, is one of the most impressive openings in New York in recent years. A hugely successful restaurateur back in Japan, Imai decided to challenge New Yorkers' expectations of Japanese cuisine in a setting which also turns cultural perceptions on their head. The principal designer is Yasumichi Morita, a young Osaka-based designer who seems to have single-handedly initiated a new style that has been called Modern Japanese Baroque. The usual light woods, polite scale and simplicity of so many sushi bars are nowhere to be seen in this glamorous, bold and very stylish fantasy for the senses. Megu covers 14,000 square feet over two floors, with a main dining room, the Kimono bar, a sushi bar, a VIP lounge and a private dining room. As Morita explains, 'Because Megu is so big, we designed it as a series of different scenes', all of which help to surprise even the wealthiest Tribeca starlets and the shyest celebs with a combination of modern luxury, high style and privacy. The restaurant even has valet parking – such a rarity in New York. It is expensive, but that's to be expected when the offerings include Kobe beef that melts in the mouth and saké-steamed abalone in *ganseki* sauce, prepared with great precision by the team of 25 chefs. Megu also has the longest and most sophisticated saké list that you're likely to find outside Japan. With a nod to the restaurant's cross-cultural status, the list has been put together by the Japan-based American expert John Gauntner.

IN THE MIX: SAKÉ

IT IS THE MAN WHO DRINKS THE FIRST BOTTLE OF SAKÉ, THEN THE SECOND BOTTLE DRINKS THE FIRST, & FINALLY IT IS THE SAKÉ THAT DRINKS THE MAN
JAPANESE PROVERB

SAKÉ, THE NATIONAL DRINK OF JAPAN, HAS BEEN AROUND SINCE WET RICE CULTIVATION BEGAN IN AROUND THE THIRD CENTURY. IN ONE OF THOSE HAPPY ACCIDENTS OF NATURE, AIRBORNE SPORES MAKE EXPOSED RICE MOULDY, & WHEN YEAST FALLS ON THE MASH, IT CREATES AN INTOXICATING MIXTURE. PRESUMABLY THIS WAS FIRST EATEN BY A FEARLESS FOOL. HAVING EVOLVED INTO RICE WINE, SAKÉ IS USUALLY DRUNK WARM, BUT EXPENSIVE, HIGH-QUALITY SAKÉ IS SERVED CHILLED TO ENHANCE THE FLAVOURS, WHICH OFTEN INCLUDE FRUIT NOTES. IT'S COMMONLY SERVED NEAT, BUT RESTAURANTS SUCH AS HAKKASAN IN LONDON HAVE BROUGHT ABOUT THE POPULARITY OF COCKTAIL CREATIONS SUCH AS THE SAKÉTINI, A MARTINI WHERE SAKÉ REPLACES VERMOUTH. THERE IS A HUGE VARIETY OF SAKÉ LABEL DESIGNS, RANGING FROM THE MORE TRADITIONAL, SUCH AS 'KYOKUCHI', WHICH NORMALLY HAVE NO ENGLISH ON THEM, TO THE HUMOROUS, SUCH AS 'DARUMA' WITH ITS PICTURE OF A ZEN MONK, & THE MORE MODERN. THE YONETSURU BREWERY WANTS ITS 'FORMULA ONE' BRAND TO BE ASSOCIATED WITH THE HIGH-OCTANE GLAMOUR OF MOTOR RACING.

The play on traditional perceptions of Japan begins outside, where passers-by can see the red sun and white background of the Japanese flag re-created by a wall made up of columns of porcelain saké bottles and rice bowls. Inside, a landing is dominated by a large, illuminated artwork which on closer inspection turns out to be a grid of saké bottle labels. Before we are barely even through the door, Yasumicha Morita wittily subverts both the increasingly outmoded, Western perception of Japan as a serious and restrained culture, and the gravity with which we sometimes approach art. The vibrant, red and mirrored Kimono bar is another alluring surprise. Rolls of kimono material are stacked to create two of the walls, while squares of patterned material form a colourful patchwork on the ceiling: the classic clothing of Japan is used to create the decoration, but we are reintroduced to it in an unusual form. The linearity of the rolls of kimonos gives a sense of speed, as if they are trails of light caught on slowly exposed film. The mirrors add to the peculiar spatial effect, helping to confound one's expectations of the usual dynamics of a barroom

MEGU, NEW YORK

MEGU
62 THOMAS STREET,
NEW YORK,
NY 10013, USA

TEL +1 212 964 7777
WWW.MEGUNYC.COM

EQUIPPED WITH STYLE:
SHAZA BY KEN TAKEYAMA

KEN TAKEYAMA DREW ON THE JAPANESE CULTURAL IMPORTANCE OF BOTH TEA & BAMBOO FOR HIS SHAZA COCKTAIL GLASS DESIGN FOR BOMBAY SAPPHIRE: 'THE MARTINI GLASS I DESIGNED EXPRESSES THE DIGNIFIED IMPRESSION OF DRY GIN THROUGH THE HARMONY OF GLASS & BAMBOO, & THE LIGHT GOING THROUGH THEM. *CHASEN* (THE TOOL USED TO STIR JAPANESE TEA) IS THE KEY DESIGN MOTIF.'

The main dining room occupies a grand, 40-foot-high room, centred on a huge, 700-pound bell – copied from one in a temple in Nara – which is suspended above a massive ice sculpture of the Buddha that has to be replaced daily. Perhaps this is a reference to Buddhist reincarnation, or mirrors the overindulging customers melting down in their seats as they consume too much fine saké and exquisite food. The bell is lit from within by vermilion light, while its design reoccurs in a scaled-down form for the shades of a four-armed lighting feature. Japanese bamboo mats find a new use as part of the wall decoration, while, in a section of the Imperial Lounge, mirrors are used to create a vortex of beautifully decorated lanterns.

Imai travelled the breadth of the United States looking for the right suppliers for his dramatic, innovative dishes, while Morita has spared no less attention to detail in forcing us to re-evaluate our perceptions of Japan. One suspects that bold new creations from both of them are to become a feature of the New York restaurant scene.

ONE ALDWYCH

Many hotel lobby bars – so often badly designed thoroughfares for unadventurous hotel guests or for travelling businessmen to have perched, impromptu meetings – were once anathemas to pleasure. That has changed radically over the last 10 years, with hotel bars leading the crème de la crème of the London bar scene and providing impressive backdrops for the revival of cocktail culture. The design of the bar has become one of the most important features of new hotel design – it is the public signpost for the ambitions of a hotel, and its success is the monitor of stylistic kudos. The Lobby Bar at One Aldwych is one of the leaders of the hotel-bar revolution, having established the popularity on which the reputation of a hotel can hang. Importantly, it achieved the Holy Grail of becoming a favourite haunt for style-conscious Londoners as well as visitors, providing year-round revenue and ensuring that it avoids that off-season, morgue-on-a-Sunday feeling that can hit hotel bars.

Named 'probably the best hotel lobby bar in London' by the *Evening Standard* and one of the top five hotel bars in the world by the *Sunday Telegraph*, the bar's grand, historical setting makes it a perfect place for classic cocktails. However, the drinks' menu includes many innovations, especially within its list of over 40 Martinis, led by the Tamarillo Martini which was awarded Best Cocktail in London by *Forbes* magazine. (You get the picture – if there's an award to be had, One Aldwych has probably already had it.) The house specialities include the Fig Martini and Below Passion Martini as well as a good range of champagnes.

CLASSIC COCKTAILS:
THE DRY MARTINI

THE TWO MAJOR & NO DOUBT APOCRYPHAL THEORIES ABOUT THE ORIGIN OF THE MARTINI BOTH INVOLVE A WEST COAST GOLD MINER. ONE HAS A BARMAN IN THE CALIFORNIAN TOWN OF MARTINEZ (THUS THE NAME) CREATING A DRINK ON THE SPUR OF THE MOMENT FOR AN OLD GOLD MINER WHO HAS BURST INTO THE BAR TO CELEBRATE HIS SUDDEN GOOD FORTUNE. HOWEVER, THE SAN FRANCISCAN BARMAN JERRY THOMAS ALSO CLAIMED TO HAVE INVENTED IT FOR A GOLD MINER ON HIS WAY TO MARTINEZ. ONE THING IS FOR SURE, THE ORIGINAL TASTED NOTHING LIKE THE DRY MARTINI OF TODAY, CONTAINING SEVERAL PARTS SWEET VERMOUTH TO ONE PART OLD TOM GIN, WHICH WAS ALSO SWEET. OVER THE YEARS, BOTH THE VERMOUTH & THE GIN WERE REPLACED BY DRY EQUIVALENTS & THE GIN BECAME THE LARGER COMPONENT. THE 'CLASSIC' BALANCE IS NOW COMMONLY FIVE PARTS GIN TO ONE VERMOUTH, BUT SOME RELEGATE THE VERMOUTH TO JUST A COUPLE OF DROPS. THE QUALITY OF THE GIN IS ESSENTIAL, WITH MANY BARTENDERS PREFERRING BOMBAY SAPPHIRE DUE TO THE SPICEY DEPTH OF ITS TASTE.

INGREDIENTS:
75 ML (2.5 OZ) BOMBAY SAPPHIRE GIN
10 ML (0.3 OZ) MARTINI EXTRA DRY VERMOUTH

METHOD:
STIR WITH ICE & STRAIN
GLASS: MARTINI
GARNISH: LEMON ZEST OR OLIVE

One of the benefits of the Lobby Bar is that it is inside such a glorious building, featuring a copper cupola dome atop a distinctive, curved corner. Another is that, although it is a lobby, it isn't a thoroughfare, inhabiting a stunning, double-height room of its own just off the hotel reception. The narrow, triangular-shaped One Aldwych building is one of the most important Edwardian designs in London, and it is now protected by English Heritage. Built in 1907 by Charles Mewès and Arthur Davis, the architects of the Ritz hotels in Paris and London, it was constructed as the offices of the now defunct national newspaper, the *Morning Post*, before becoming a bank. Partially clad in Norwegian granite, the exterior combines British neoclassicism with typically Parisian decoration including swags, balustrades and ironwork. Due to the involvement of Mewès and Davis, the conversion into a hotel feels like something of a homecoming for the building.

THE MIXOLOGIST: ANDREW PENGELLY

ANDREW PENGELLY IS ONE OF LONDON'S MOST INFLUENTIAL BARTENDERS. OVER THE LAST 12 YEARS HE HAS BEEN PERFECTING HIS CRAFT AT SOME OF THE UK'S TOP COCKTAIL BARS INCLUDING TITANIC, ZINC & CIRCUS. CURRENTLY HE IS BAR MANAGER AT THE ACCLAIMED CHINA TANG AT THE DORCHESTER HOTEL IN LONDON. WHEN PASSING ON HIS EXPERT KNOWLEDGE TO ASPIRING BARTENDERS, PENGELLY IS A STRONG ADVOCATE OF THE CLASSIC COCKTAIL PHILOSOPHY. 'CLASSICS ARE CLASSICS BECAUSE THEY REMEMBER CERTAIN RULES. FIRSTLY, USE ONLY THE FINEST INGREDIENTS. SECONDLY, KEEP IT SIMPLE. IT'S TRUE THAT LESS IS MORE. & FINALLY, RESPECT YOUR BASE SPIRIT. BALANCE YOUR FLAVOURS & NEVER, NEVER ALLOW ONE INGREDIENT TO OVERPOWER THE FLAVOUR OF ANOTHER.' ONE OF HIS PERSONAL FAVOURITES IS A CLASSIC MARTINI COCKTAIL, MADE WITH BOMBAY SAPPHIRE WHICH HE REFERS TO AS, 'QUITE SIMPLY A MIXOLOGIST'S DREAM'. 'THE BOMBAY SAPPHIRE CLASSIC MARTINI COCKTAIL WITH AN OLIVE IS THE PERFECT SHOWCASE FOR ALL 10 BOTANICALS & THE EXCEPTIONALLY SMOOTH TASTE OF BOMBAY SAPPHIRE. IT'S A COCKTAIL MASTERPIECE.'

The Lobby Bar is in the former advertisement hall and is blessed by the room's tremendous, almost cathedral-like dimensions and some of its original features. Double-height windows and oak panelling give the room elegance and grandeur, but the contemporary, clean interior prevents it feeling too fussy and traditional. Part of the contemporary edge comes from large sculptures, including *The Boatman* by Andre Wallace, a huge wooden oarsman who introduces customers to the room with his oars raised as if to say, 'That's enough work for the day'. The hotel exhibits over 300 artworks, with each guestroom featuring an original piece. Other contemporary touches in the bar include huge Perspex plinths supporting flower displays, and bespoke furniture, most notably the incredibly high-backed Push-Me Pull-Me armchairs that match the perpendicular grandeur of the room. High wooden stools stand before the polished sheen

IN THE MIX: THE THIN MAN

'THE IMPORTANT THING IS THE RHYTHM. ALWAYS HAVE RHYTHM IN YOUR SHAKING. NOW A MANHATTAN YOU ALWAYS SHAKE TO FOX-TROT TIME, A BRONX TO TWO-STEP TIME, A DRY MARTINI YOU ALWAYS SHAKE TO WALTZ TIME.' – NICK CHARLES, *THE THIN MAN* (1932) BASED ON DASHIELL HAMMETT'S COMIC DETECTIVE NOVEL, *THE THIN MAN* IS ONE OF THE GREAT MARTINI MOVIES, WITH THE GENTLEMAN-DETECTIVE NICK CHARLES (PLAYED BY WILLIAM POWELL) FINDING EVERY OPPORTUNITY FOR A DRY QUIP & A DRY MARTINI.

ONE ALDWYCH, LONDON

LOBBY BAR
ONE ALDWYCH,
LONDON WC2B 4RH, UK

TEL +44 (0)20 7300 1070
WWW.ONEALDWYCH.COM

of the Lobby Bar's counter: a dark, graceful and stately arc with its bottle display set into a huge internal window. The furniture in the centre of the room, which has a limestone floor and white, ribbed pillars, includes miniature armchairs, comfortable two-seater sofas and small wooden tables, providing an intimate scale within the grandiosity. The room has a genuine buzz, perhaps because it carries the memory of the clatter and chatter of copywriters from a former age.

SCARLET

Singapore, home of the famous Singapore Sling, is a city on the move. It's a city that has reinvented itself in recent times with a new focus for tourism, finance and impressive architecture. Although it took some time for the leisure industry to catch up with the boom, there is a burgeoning new breed of hotels, restaurants and bars which are now putting excellent design and menus to the forefront of the city's attractions. This is typified none more so than by The Scarlet, with a range of bars and restaurants that have become a magnet for food and drink lovers as well travellers seeking an intimate, rather sensual refuge in an excellent location.

The restaurants and bars are not a mere add-on to the hotel's services: they shout out for attention beyond the walls of the hotel. Their names — Desire, Breeze and Bold — have an audacity about them (as do the five different guestroom types: Splendour, Passion, Opulent, Lavish and Swank). Bold, the bar, is true to its name, carrying a darkly sensuous but surprising attitude through its furnishings, which include incredibly high-backed, black leather chairs, suede banquettes by Dadar and a black-and-white-patterned sofa with armrests that reach up high enough to become a back support. The furniture is dressed with velvet and ostrich leather cushions in red and gold to add extra comfort and opulence. The soft fabrics are offset by smoked-mirror ceilings and Porto Oro marble. The bar has quickly become a destination for drinks aficionados and fashionistas to partake of an extensive list of cocktails, whiskies and canapés.

SCARLET, SINGAPORE

THE SCARLET
33 ERSKINE ROAD,
SINGAPORE 069333

TEL +65 6511 3333
WWW.THESCARLETHOTEL.COM

THE DESIGNER: MICHAEL TAN

MICHAEL TAN, THE CONCEPT DIRECTOR FOR THE SCARLET HOTEL, DREW HIS INSPIRATION FROM A PIECE OF CHENILLE FROM RUSSELL & HARVEY: 'WHEN I SAW THE SWATCH, IT BECAME THE FIRST PIECE ON THE GAMEBOARD TO DEVELOP A SENSUOUS, DRAMATIC ENVIRONMENT THAT HITS YOU AS SOON AS YOU WALK IN THE DOOR. WE WANTED PEOPLE TO EXPERIENCE A RICH, EXCITING AMBIENCE.'

Desire provides the formal restaurant experience, while Breeze is an outdoor bar and restaurant. Set on a terrace on top of the renovated Art Deco wing of the Scarlet, Breeze features the building's original pavilion, Dedon daybeds and Chengai timber decking for those who wish to enjoy Mediterranean cuisine or cocktails while overlooking the sloping terracotta roofs of the surrounding 19th-century district. Desire has an Absoluto Nero stone counter and white stone flooring, silver pillars, shimmering curtains and a changing LED light display which sets different moods throughout the day. Perhaps the restaurant's most distinctive features are Ernest Chan's artworks, which make a sexual adventure out of the shape of the capsicum plant, and the fuchsia chairs with a back formed from three descending circles, reminiscent of traditional Far Eastern architecture.

Many of the best European and American bars and restaurants that have balanced innovative food and drinks with innovative design have an Asian influence — Scarlet has turned that on its head, cherry-picking successful elements of overseas lifestyle-culture and giving them a Singaporean makeover. The interiors deliberately incorporate

CLASSIC COCKTAILS:
THE SINGAPORE SLING

THE SCARLET HOTEL MAY BE POPULAR BECAUSE OF ITS ARRAY OF MORE MODERN COCKTAILS, BUT SINGAPORE WILL ALWAYS BE ASSOCIATED WITH THE COCKTAIL CREATION OF ANOTHER HOTEL BAR. THE SINGAPORE SLING, INVENTED AT THE LONG BAR AT THE RAFFLES HOTEL BY NGIAM TONG BOON IN 1910, HAS BECOME ONE OF THE CLASSIC GIN COCKTAILS. THERE ARE MANY VARIANTS, OFTEN INCLUDING CLUB SODA, BUT THIS IS MORE OR LESS THE ORIGINAL AS STILL SERVED AT THE LONG BAR.

INGREDIENTS:
30 ML (1 OZ) GIN
5 ML (0.25 OZ) CHERRY BRANDY
5 ML (0.25 OZ) LEMON JUICE
5 ML (0.25 OZ) PINEAPPLE JUICE
5 ML (0.25 OZ) TRIPLE SEC
5 ML (0.25 OZ) BENEDICTINE
SMALL DASH OF GRENADINE
DASH OF BITTERS
TOPPED WITH CHILLED SODA

METHOD:
SHAKE WITH ICE & STRAIN
GLASS: COLLINS
GARNISH: CHERRY & SLICE
OF PINEAPPLE

stylistic elements of Singapore's architectural heritage along with the blend of contemporary and traditional opulence which is often the mark of the European boutique hotels and high-class restaurants. Throughout, the design has a red (thus the name Scarlet) and gold signature which is used with black to maintain a restrained, Eastern elegance. Each area, though, has a unique feel, from the lobby with its Bisazza mosaics, Russell & Harvey fabrics and Maharam gold wall-coverings, to guestrooms with, variously, Galaxy or Absoluto Nero granite features, black marble bathrooms, and Harrison and Gill mirrors.

Grace International, who both conceptualized and developed the Scarlet, spent $35 million on realizing the project — a tremendous outlay on an 84-room hotel. However, the three restaurants and bars have their own independent vibrancy and local appeal, giving the venture a sure-footed confidence that the investment will be recouped. A Singaporean company, Grace plans to step abroad with European and American initiatives. Its attention to detail in its food and drinks spaces will serve it well.

GRAN HOTEL DOMINE

The Guggenheim Museum's turning of Bilbao from a seemingly uninspiring industrial city into a cultural destination is so significant that the phrase 'the Bilbao effect' has slipped into common usage to paraphrase how an iconic new building can change the fortunes of a city. Opening in 1997, Frank O. Gehry's building, with its curving peels of titanium, as well as the modern art exhibitions it houses, has attracted art and design lovers like moths to a flame. The rest of the city needed to catch up to truly benefit from its new attraction, but in 2003 the Gran Hotel Domine Bilbao opened to give those culture vultures the perfect place to stay. Fortunately, though, it's not just a tourist haven, with locals also stopping by to eat, drink and play.

With an interior created by leading Spanish designers Javier Mariscal and Fernando Salas, the hotel is a living exhibition of the best in European 20th-century design, and a fitting cousin to the nearby Guggenheim which is reflected in its black-mirrored exterior. The lobby announces the hotel's grand intentions, with Mariscal's 26-metre-tall *Fossil Cypress* sculpture, weighing 90 tonnes and soaring up the atrium, along with his huge, red, figure-of-eight sofa. One of the hotel's highlights is the Metropol café and bar, a monument to Bauhaus design from the 1920s. Taking inspiration from the work of Walter Gropius and Mies van der Rohe, the scheme is almost entirely black, white and stainless steel. The space has a geometry and stylish severity which is carried

through by the black Cesca chairs, patterned floor, and even the placemats. The huge windows overlook Jeff Koons' immense *Puppy* flower-sculpture as well as the Guggenheim.

By contrast, the Splash & Crash cocktail bar is a tribute to design classics from the 1960s and 1970s. The white, silver and red décor is retro-futuristic and includes such classics as Ron Arad's Little Albert chairs and Eero Saarinen's stools and tables. They are accompanied by white leather sofas and Mariscal's comfortable, black-and-white Alessandra armchairs which are inspired by organic forms. Artwork includes two Pop images of 'Splash' and 'Crash'. The bar counter is a clinical, silver metal arc set into a linked-metal wall, while shelving and further seating are cusped around a series of angled white columns that give the impression of some alien, futuristic forest.

EQUIPPED WITH STYLE: CYLINDA-LINE BARWARE BY ARNE JACOBSEN

WORK BY DANISH DESIGNER ARNE JACOBSEN (1902–71) IS NECESSARILY INCLUDED IN GRAN HOTEL DOMINE BILBAO'S COLLECTION OF ICONIC 20TH-CENTURY DESIGNS. HIS SIMPLE BUT INNOVATIVE SWAN & EGG CHAIRS ARE ENDURING CLASSICS WHICH FEATURE IN MANY STYLE-LED HOTEL, BAR & OFFICE INTERIORS, WHILE HIS CYLINDA-LINE TABLEWARE SERIES, WITH STAINLESS-STEEL CYLINDRICAL BODIES & BAKELITE HANDLES, HAS ALSO BECOME ICONIC. IN 2004, STELTON (WWW.STELTON.COM) LAUNCHED A LIMITED EDITION, STERLING SILVER VERSION OF THE CYLINDA BARWARE (PICTURED), INCLUDING A MARTINI MIXER & SPOON, SHAKER & ICE BUCKET.

The hotel's more formal eatery is Beltz The Black, a Basque restaurant which has a private area with two glass walls looking onto the lobby. In sympathy with the Basque liking for simple, natural tastes, the cuisine of acclaimed chef Ramón Berriozabal is complemented by a minimalist design with a reliance on natural materials such as oak and featuring a wall made up of shards of stone.

Hotel guests have a series of other advantages beyond the public spaces and their rooms, which have bathrooms with items by some of the superstar designers of recent times including Philippe Starck, Jasper Morrison, Alvar Aalto and Arne Jacobsen. The Buenasvistas terrace provides Bilbao's ultimate cocktail spot, with unrivalled views of the Guggenheim Museum, the city and the countryside beyond, while the Txoko Tranquilo reading corner is a design lover's heaven. Its library is stacked with titles on architecture, design and

GRAN HOTEL DOMINE, BILBAO

GRAN HOTEL DOMINE
ALAMEDA DE MAZARREDO,
61, 48009 BILBAO, SPAIN

TEL +34 944 253 300
WWW.HOTELES-SILKEN.COM/GHDB

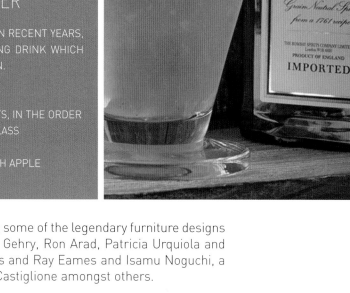

INSPIRED CREATIONS:
SAPPHIRE POM-POM BY JAMIE WALKER

APPLE MARTINI COCKTAILS MAY HAVE BEEN ALL THE RAGE IN RECENT YEARS, BUT MIXOLOGIST JAMIE WALKER HAS CREATED A NEW LONG DRINK WHICH PLAYS ON THE COMPLEMENTARY SYNTHESIS OF APPLE & GIN.

INGREDIENTS:
35 ML (1 OZ) BOMBAY SAPPHIRE GIN
25 ML (0.75 OZ) FRESH APPLE JUICE
50 ML (1.5 OZ) BASQUE CIDER
DASH OF LEMON JUICE
DASH OF THYME-INFUSED SYRUP

METHOD:
BUILD THE INGREDIENTS, IN THE ORDER AS LISTED, INTO THE GLASS
GLASS: HIGHBALL
GARNISH: FAN OF FRESH APPLE

interiors, which can be perused in a setting featuring some of the legendary furniture designs of the 20th century. Chairs by Harry Bertoia, Frank Gehry, Ron Arad, Patricia Urquiola and Mariscal vie for attention amongst tables by Charles and Ray Eames and Isamu Noguchi, a vase by Aalto and lighting by Jacobsen and Achille Castiglione amongst others.

Gran Hotel Domine Bilbao, or GHDB as it is more simply known, has pulled off the trick of matching the desires, aspirations and interests of local people and stylish visitors alike. Initially, many people were surprised that such a temple to quality and design was part of the Silken group, known for decent but largely unremarkable hotels. However, 2005 saw the group hire 18 of the world's leading designers to collaborate on the Hotel Puerta América in Madrid. Norman Foster, Zaha Hadid, Ron Arad, Jean Nouvel et al lined up alongside the GHDB's Mariscal and Salas to design a floor each. Silken has clearly seen that although it can often cost more, innovative design can reap rewards.

ESTABLISHMENT

The Establishment, with its hub of bars and restaurants, is a magnet for Sydney stylites who have been heading to the Hemmesphere private members' club, Est restaurant, the Tank Stream bar or the Establishment Bar itself since its opening in 2000. Fashionableness, rather than popularity, is often linked to bespoke creations and unique environments. It should have been a tough call for Justin and Bettina Hemmes of the Merivale Group, which was originally a fashion house, to make a star attraction out of what is essentially a complex. In design terms, they have pulled it off by giving each bar or restaurant a very distinctive style which is carried through by a different ambience. Fortunately, there is nothing corporate or run-of-the-mill about any of the individual ventures within the Establishment.

The bars, restaurants and hotel of the Establishment were converted from George Patterson House, a rather grand colonial building which had been damaged by fire in 1996. A six-storey tower has been added to the building but some of the glories of the original structure have been incorporated or even emphasised to good effect. The Establishment Bar, the largest of the drinking venues, is a tall white room with a colonnade of cast-iron columns with Corinthian capitals. The decorated, pressed-metal ceiling, modern chandeliers and 42-metre, white marble bar counter, which runs the length of the room, help to give it a simple but stately elegance. The bar leads out into the glass-covered garden courtyard, where the scarred and burnt walls and pillars have been deliberately left to contrast with the interior's refinement and to serve as a reminder of the building's previous misadventure.

On a far more intimate scale, the Tank Stream bar has its own entrance on Tank Stream Way. Situated in the original storage area of George Patterson House, the bar takes its name from a freshwater stream – which played an important part in the initial settlement of Sydney – that runs underneath. The design incorporates the storehouse's dark-stained timber ceiling. Rough, unpainted pillars and whitewashed brickwork create a textural contrast to the stone flooring, the crisp, linear furnishings and the bookshelf-like, square grid of the bottle display. Close to the Australian Stock Exchange, the bar seems to be a favourite with stylish financiers, who choose from a menu of classic cocktails with an emphasis on quality spirits, such as the French Martini with Bombay Sapphire.

Getting past the bouncers and into the Establishment bar can be a feat, but real exclusivity is the preserve of Hemmesphere. The private lounge is a sultry, North African enclave filled with ottomans and divans strewn with cushions, along with leather armchairs that add a traditional club feel. It lounge has its place in the cigar revival, with a custom-designed humidor and an extensive list of Cuban cigars. Hemmesphere, which is continuing to win best bar awards, is also the cocktail heart of the Establishment, with a good, long list of innovative creations, including the Hemmesphere signature cocktail: Grand Marnier liqueur, Hennessy VS cognac, Massenez Pêche liqueur, guava and lime juice. The ceilings of the main room are high, but the walls are covered in warm fabrics to increase the feeling of mellowness and intimacy.

EQUIPPED WITH STYLE:
COSMO SHAKER BY MARC NEWSON

MARC NEWSON, AUSTRALIA'S MOST FAMOUS DESIGNER WHO WAS BORN IN SYDNEY IN 1963, CREATED THE COSMO COCKTAIL SHAKER FOR ALESSI IN 2003. DESIGNED IN CONSULTATION WITH ALBERTO GOZZI, IT HAS A FLUTED CRYSTAL MAIN BODY, RATHER THAN THE MORE USUAL SMOOTH STAINLESS STEEL, WITH A CHOICE OF CAPS IN BLUE OR BLACK. THE COSMO IS PICTURED HERE WITH THE BOLLY WINE COOLER BY JASPER MORRISON, ONE OF BRITAIN'S LEADING PRODUCT DESIGNERS, & STEFANO GIOVANNONI'S MAMI MARTINI GLASS. NEWSON'S RECENT VENTURES INCLUDE INTERIORS FOR HOTEL PUERTA AMÉRICA IN MADRID & THE LEVER HOUSE RESTAURANT IN NEW YORK.

ESTABLISHMENT, SYDNEY

THE ESTABLISHMENT
252 GEORGE STREET,
SYDNEY 2000, AUSTRALIA

TEL +61 (02) 9240 3000
WWW.MERIVALE.COM

CLASSIC COCKTAILS: TOM COLLINS

HEMMESPHERE AT THE ESTABLISHMENT OFFERS TAILOR-MADE COCKTAIL WORKSHOPS TO MEET THE GROWING DEMAND & INTEREST IN COCKTAILS. ONE OF THE ESSENTIAL COCKTAILS THAT ANY WOULD-BE MIXOLOGIST, BAR CHEF OR COCKTAILIAN SHOULD PERFECT EARLY ON IS THE TOM COLLINS. ORIGINALLY, THE 19TH-CENTURY JOHN COLLINS, POSSIBLY CREATED BY A WAITER AT LIMMER'S HOTEL IN LONDON, WAS MADE WITH JENEVER (DUTCH GIN) & ITS COUSIN TOM COLLINS WAS MADE WITH OLD TOM, A SWEETENED GIN. BOTH TYPES OF GIN ARE NOW RARELY IN USE. THE TOM COLLINS DEVELOPED INTO A DRY LONDON GIN CONCOCTION, WHILE THE JOHN COLLINS IS NOW MADE WITH BOURBON.

INGREDIENTS:
30 ML (1 OZ) GIN
15 ML (0.5 OZ) FRESH LEMON JUICE
SUGAR SYRUP TO TASTE

METHOD:
SHAKE WITH ICE & STRAIN. TOP WITH SODA.
GLASS: COLLINS OR HIGHBALL
GARNISH: LEMON SLICE & SPRIG OF MINT.

The Hemmesphere lounge has a sushi bar but the Establishment's fine dining restaurant is three floors below on Level One. Est., serving Peter Doyle's French-inspired cuisine, inhabits a similarly colonnaded space to the Establishment bar, but further comfort and luxury has been afforded by polished wooden floorboards, a chocolate-brown carpet and walnut furniture. Interesting features include tall, wooden floor lamps and an oversized iron birdcage which acts as the wine cellar. The restaurant, which is rated amongst the best in Sydney, also has a cocktail lounge with silk-covered walls, sofas and a marble bar counter.

Underneath all this lies the Tank nightclub, which attracts international DJs and a fairly stellar crowd. It's a two-tier space designed by Hecker Phelan and includes three bars and a private lounge which has metallic bean-bags and even more private booths. The design incorporates the 19th-century building's original timber beams and columns, augmented by huge mirror balls and contemporary wall sculptures.

SEMIRAMIS HOTEL

The lounge, bar and restaurant of the Semiramis Hotel in Athens have been buzzing with design-conscious 30-something jet-setters and Athenians since it opened in time for the 2004 Olympics. While it is feared that many of the huge developments created for the games have already become white elephants on the skyline, and that the Olympics did not really have the financial benefits expected, the hotel, bar and restaurant scene has entered a new, high-design era. Life Gallery, Fresh Hotel, Kaningos 21, the rejuvenated Balthazar, Island and 48 The Restaurant have all added to the mix, making Athens more than merely a hit-and-run stopover for cultural tourists. Semiramis, designed by Karim Rashid, is the most talked about of all the new developments.

Sitting poolside at the Semiramis, sipping a cocktail from one of Rashid's slanting glasses, is probably the single most fashionable thing you can do in Athens, not least because the pool is one of the most unusual you are ever likely to see. Rashid is famous worldwide for subverting the norm expected of household objects by combining distinctive shapes, colours and materials, and using the very latest in

manufacturing processes. Semiramis was his first hotel design, and his natural leaning towards startling innovation has not been cowed by the larger scale. Shaped like an amoeba just before the point of separation, the pool's base is covered with fluid strata of green, blue and brown Bisazza mosaic tiles. It is surrounded by timber decking and yellow terrazzo paving. One side opens up to a covered dining area in which a neon artwork and Rashid's Kab chairs help create a cutting-edge setting. The pool's distinctive shape is repeated in the restaurant's pink placemats and the blue-and-orange glass tables. The menu is international, but still holds true to its Greek locality.

Rashid calls the Semiramis a '21st-century hotel' and at times it borders on the futuristic, especially through the use of translucent, coloured Plexiglass which forms surprising divisions, angles and entranceways, including a cut-out that leads into the bar. The bar lounge features a huge bulbous form emerging from the double-height ceiling, with an orchestrated light display sparkling like the sky at night. Almost every

HALF-EGYPTIAN, HALF-ENGLISH, RAISED IN CANADA & BASED IN NEW YORK, KARIM RASHID IS A TRULY INTERNATIONAL DESIGNER. HE MADE HIS NAME IN 1996 WITH THE GARBO WASTEBASKET & FOUND GREAT SUCCESS WITH HOUSEHOLD INDUSTRIAL DESIGNS. HE HAS NOW VENTURED INTO HOTEL DESIGN WITH THE SEMIRAMIS & THE MYHOTEL GROUP, WHERE HE HAS CARRIED THROUGH A PASSION FOR INNOVATION, AMORPHOUS SHAPES & COLOURED TRANSPARENCY. HE HAS ALSO DEVELOPED A MARTINI GLASS FOR BOMBAY SAPPHIRE (PICTURED) & A RANGE OF BAR ACCESSORIES FOR COPCO. HE'S A SOMETIMES CONTROVERSIAL QUOTE MACHINE & IMPRESSIVE SELF-PUBLICIST, PUBLISHING *I WANT TO CHANGE THE WORLD* IN 2001.

single item of furniture in the hotel has been designed by Rashid, and here it includes Bloob bar stools and Spline black, white and lime-green chairs and sofas. Other pink, curving sofas interlock to create unusual, inclusive seating arrangements, while the multilayers of his Nuage glass tables can be fanned out to accommodate extra guests. Rashid is attempting to rebuild furniture arrangements to suit the social behaviour in an exciting, free-flowing cocktail bar.

The lobby lounge is made up of pink-and-white Blob chairs and distinctive black-and-white Wavelength sofas, set in lines so that the tops of their undulating back rests give the impression of a black sea. These pave the way towards a huge neon artwork, *YE$* by Tim Noble and Sue Webster. This is a perfect example of owner Dakis Joannou's and Rashid's intention to make design, art and ambience work as one within the Semiramis. Joannou, a trained architect himself and a collector of modern art, spent 23 million euros on creating the hotel, and it acts as a living gallery for part of his

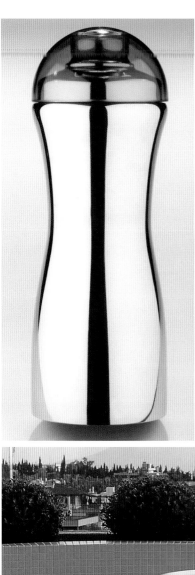

EQUIPPED WITH STYLE:
COPCO KARIM COCKTAIL SHAKER

WITH A CHOICE OF BLUE OR CHARCOAL TRANSPARENT TOPS, KARIM RASHID'S SHAKER CARRIES HIS SIGNATURE MOTIFS OF CURVES & TINTED TRANSLUCENCY. THE MAIN BODY IS DOUBLE-WALL STAINLESS STEEL WITH A 24-OUNCE CAPACITY & FEATURES A BUILT-IN STRAINER. IT'S AVAILABLE FROM WWW.TABLETOOLS.COM.

collection, including work by Jeff Koons. Even the main entranceway, a pink glass light-box, suggests a radical, contemporary art gallery rather than a hotel. However, the Semiramis is designed to be experiential, which is why its restaurants and lounges have such a strong appeal beyond the realms of hotel guests, and why – despite the high-art and high-design mix – it manages to be unpretentious.

The hotel is situated out in the green, wealthy suburb of Kifissia, but people travel to it from across Athens for the sake of a Caipirinha or two, which bodes well for Joannou's investment. Upstairs from the two floors that incorporate the lounges and restaurant, the guestrooms have been hugely acclaimed, incorporating innovative design and materials amongst the continued themes of organic shapes, coloured transparency and artworks. They also have excellent, balcony views of the surrounding countryside. Perhaps the best residencies, though, are the six poolside bungalows with their own private garden.

The Sanderson is the best-designed hotel to have emerged out of the collaboration between designer Philippe Starck and hotelier Ian Schrager. Their partnership added a new fizz to hotel culture between 1988, with the opening of the Royalton in New York, and 2002 when the partnership effectively came to an end. The Sanderson, completed in 2000, was one of their final works and the Long Bar remains its über-cool jewel. It's a hard trick to maintain popularity with the style-cognoscenti for such a sustained period, but the Long Bar is still one of London's best places in which to see and be seen. The key to the bar's longevity is found in the combination of a luxurious but surprisingly simple design and a drop-dead-gorgeous cocktail menu, including a list of exquisite Martinis. Of course, the simplicity is an apparition – the Long Bar is the product of Starck's desire to play with design, expectation and the rituals of human interaction to create something both humorous and truly innovative.

The bar is almost entirely made up of an 80-foot-long, four-sided counter surrounded by tall bar stools in the centre of a fairly narrow space. The bar counter glows with light emanating through thinly cut white onyx, with a steel lip providing room for the bar stools. One of Starck's early successes was his 1989 ornamentation of the Asahi Beer headquarters, which is amongst Tokyo's most striking modern buildings. The Long Bar draws on his interest in Japanese style, basing the counter design on a *bento* box – the traditionally rectangular lunch container. Starck removed the familiar bar detail of a raised bottle and glass display – all the bar ephemera is held below the

THE MIXOLOGIST: HENRY BESANT

STILL IN HIS EARLY 30S, HENRY BESANT HAS BEEN ASSOCIATED WITH SOME OF LONDON'S BEST COCKTAIL BARS. HE WAS THE ORIGINAL MANAGER OF BOTH THE ST MARTIN'S LANE & THE SANDERSON'S BARS, CONTRIBUTING TO THE LONG BAR'S REPUTATION FOR INNOVATIVE MARTINIS, WHICH HE SAYS WERE HELPED TO LOOK GREAT BY BEING UNDERLIT BY THE BAR'S ONYX COUNTER. HE ALSO USED MASSIVE OLIVES & 9-INCH STICKS TO COMPLEMENT STARCK'S PLAY ON EXPECTED PROPORTIONS. THE MENU AT THE LONG BAR CHANGES SEVERAL TIMES A YEAR BUT ONE OF BESANT'S ORIGINAL CLASSICS IS LIKELY TO ALWAYS REMAIN THE SANDERSON MARTINI, THE BAR'S SIGNATURE DRINK CONSISTING OF LEMON VODKA, CUCUMBER VODKA, BROWN SUGAR, APPLE JUICE & FRESH GRAPES. HE SAYS THAT THE KEY TO A SUCCESSFUL BAR 'INVOLVES A SPIRIT OF INDEPENDENCE' & THAT YOU MUST 'MAKE YOUR PRODUCT REALLY GOOD & NOT JUST FASHIONABLE: GOOD DRINKS, GOOD SERVICE, GOOD DESIGN'. AFTER LEAVING THE LONG BAR, HE SET UP THE TRAFALGAR'S ROCKWELL HOTEL BAR & HELPED CREATE THE LONSDALE'S REPUTATION AS ONE OF THE BEST COCKTAIL BARS IN LONDON. HIS LATEST VENTURES INCLUDE ALL STAR LANES, A BOUTIQUE BOWLING ALLEY, RESTAURANT & BAR THAT SPECIALISES IN AMERICAN FOOD & COCKTAILS. HE ALSO RUNS THE WORLDWIDE COCKTAIL CLUB, A CENTRE OF EXCELLENCE WHICH ADVISES NEW BARS ON COCKTAIL MENUS, TRAINING & DESIGN.

level of the counter, emphasising the idea of a solid rectangular box and also allowing patrons to have an uninterrupted view of each other across the counter. Consequently, the whole bar is a playground for social interplay – everybody can see everybody else. The white-leather bar stools also allude to the sexual play: the back of each is stamped with Ramak Fazel's photographic image of a huge female eye. Eyes are also a major feature of the few portraits, including one of a white bulldog with a black eye patch, that decorate the walls.

Unlike the Light Bar at Schrager's other London hotel, St Martin's Lane, or the Sanderson's own Purple Bar, the Long Bar is a public bar where there's no need to be on the guest list. The whole design relies on a subtle combination of exclusivity and accessibility. The street-side wall has floor-to-ceiling glazing, but this is dressed with white drapes that largely obscure the interior: it's a tantalising invitation. Inside, the drapes protect the revellers from

LONG BAR, LONDON

LONG BAR
SANDERSON HOTEL,
50 BERNERS ST,
LONDON, W1T 3NG, UK

TEL +44 (0)20 7300 1400
WWW.SANDERSONHOTEL.COM

EQUIPPED WITH STYLE:
JUICY SALIF BY PHILIPPE STARCK

CREATED IN 1990 BY FRENCH DESIGNER PHILIPPE STARCK, THE JUICY SALIF BECAME AN ICON OF HOUSEHOLD OBJECT DESIGN & HELPED TURN STARCK INTO A SUPERSTAR. PRODUCED BY ALESSI, THE ALUMINIUM LEMON SQUEEZER ESTABLISHED STARCK'S TRADEMARK OF PLAYING WITH PERCEPTIONS BY COMBINING SEEMINGLY UNCONNECTED ASSOCIATIONS WITHIN ONE OBJECT – SO A SQUEEZER IS ALSO A SCULPTURAL OBJECT THAT CONJURES IMAGES OF SPACE ROCKETS OR ALIEN SPIDERS. STARCK HAS LONG HELD A VISION OF DEMOCRATISING HIGH DESIGN THROUGH AFFORDABLE OBJECTS, & THE LOW PRICE & GOOD AVAILABILITY OF THE JUICY SALIF BROUGHT HIS WORK TO THE ATTENTION OF A WIDE PUBLIC. HIS OTHER COMMERCIALLY AVAILABLE BAR EPHEMERA INCLUDES MIAMIAM GLASSES FOR DRIADE & THE RATHER LESS AFFORDABLE ROYALTON BAR STOOLS, DESIGNED FOR HIS FIRST IAN SCHRAGER HOTEL PROJECT.

prying eyes, but also emphasise the feeling of a light, unconstrained space. The other long wall is also fully glazed and includes doors onto the interior courtyard garden, a beautiful survivor from the building's original 1958 design when it was constructed to house the headquarters of the Sanderson fabric company. Designed by Philip Hicks and now classified as a 'Heritage Garden', it is also inspired by Japanese design.

The Purple Bar is a totally different concoction from the Long Bar. Accessible through a small door in the centre of the lobby, it is an Alice in Wonderland-inspired grotto in which Starck plays with conventions. Featuring miniature Queen Anne chairs, purple wall coverings and a monolithic bar counter made from a hunk of granite, the bar is a seductive, private enclave for hotel guests and celebrities seeking an alternative to the show-and-tell atmosphere of the Long Bar.

FIRE & AGNI

Fire and Agni, the highly acclaimed restaurant and bar, not only share a linked design within the Park Hotel in New Delhi, but also really have the same name. 'Agni' is Sanskrit for fire, and it also has a religious connotation as the name of an important god in Vedic mythology. While the restaurant draws on fire for cooking, the bar draws on Agni for a sense of energy and purity. The fire connection is highly suitable, as together Fire and Agni are as hot as hot can be, forming the hub of the increasingly design-conscious Delhi scene. Ever since they opened in 2004, they have been amongst the very best nightspots in the whole of India, and are even compared favourably to the fashionista-nests of Mumbai, the city everyone points to as the country's entertainment and style capital. You only have to step into Agni for a second at around midnight to feel its sophisticated, buzzing energy, fuelled by the growing economic and cultural confidence of India.

The Park has been open since 1987 but has recently undergone a design transformation inspired by the five elements. British company Conran & Partners have enthused Fire and Agni with a highly developed fire motif which includes the obvious presence of flames and the more subtle introduction of warm materials and lighting effects. Entrance to the bar, Agni, is through a curtain of glass beads – a last shower of water before you enter the furnace. A firewall made of bronze introduces the theme, while the room itself radiates with an orange glow. Walnut flooring and

panelling is used to create a sophisticated warmth. A bright yellow-orange wall, criss-crossed by a trellis of bronze strips, creates a glow behind a divan-style leather banquette adorned with cushions in complementary shades of gold, brown and cream. Other furnishings include brown leather tub chairs with curving wooden backs, along with round, glass-topped tables that are lit from within to create a glowing orange surface. These glowing tables could come across as too gimmicky for a bar as refined as Agni, but the idea has been executed in an interesting and stylish manner, while the whole design is so well considered that the more individual, showy sparks of design creativity are always supported by a stylish, intelligent grace. This is true of the panel of illuminated licks of flame that runs behind the length of the 35-foot bar counter (which, like the tables, features a glowing orange surface). While a strip of real-flame effect would have been corny, the flames are two-dimensional cut-outs that combine high-design and cartoonish qualities. Sandwiched between the dark, textured counter front and the reserved stateliness of the above-bar walnut panelling, the result is sophisticated in a humorous, knowing way.

INSPIRED CREATIONS:
DELHI SAPPHIRE BY JAMIE WALKER

JAMIE WALKER EVOKES THE FLAVOURS OF INDIA WITH A NEW COCKTAIL
THAT COMBINES HOME-GROWN POMEGRANATE, GRAPES & MANGO WITH GIN
& GRAND MARNIER.

INGREDIENTS:
50 ML (1.5 OZ) BOMBAY SAPPHIRE GIN
15 ML (0.5 OZ) GRAND MARNIER
5 SWEET WHITE GRAPES
30 ML (1 OZ) FRESH MANGO JUICE
25 ML (0.75 OZ) POMEGRANATE JUICE
SQUEEZE OF FRESH LIME

METHOD:
MUDDLE THE GRAPES, SHAKE ALL
THE INGREDIENTS WITH ICE &
STRAIN TWICE
GLASS: MARTINI
GARNISH: WEDGE OF LIME

The design ethos of Agni extends to the emphasis on a good range of new and classic cocktails, made by bar staff in bespoke uniforms designed by Rohit Bal, and an all-day menu of Indian food with a contemporary twist. At night DJs play live sets of world music and the dance floor at the end of the bar teems with a blend of international jet-setters and Delhi's own high-heeled highbrows.

Next door to Agni, the 60-seater Fire restaurant also specialises in Indian cuisine and continues the flame theme of Agni. The other side of the same wall of fire that runs behind the counter in the bar takes pride of place within the design of the restaurant space, which generally leans towards greater elegance. The panels of fire are semitransparent, so diners can see an array of the bar display bottles amongst the flames or glimpse the movement of a shadow. Walnut panelling is used again to encase the fire display, but the mood of the rest of the room is lighter, with a limestone floor and pale ochre tones for the furnishings. The room is lit with hundreds of individual clear bulbs suspended from the ceiling to create a hail of

FIRE & AGNI, NEW DEHLI

FIRE & AGNI
THE PARK HOTEL,
15 PARLIAMENT STREET,
NEW DELHI 110 001, INDIA

TEL +91 (0)11 2374 3000
WWW.THEPARKHOTELS.COM

IN THE MIX: LONDON GIN

TO CREATE A LONDON-STYLE GIN A NEUTRAL GRAIN SPIRIT IS PRODUCED FROM A GRAIN MASH. THE PURER THE SPIRIT IS, THE BETTER. THE GIN'S FLAVOUR IS THEN ASSIGNED BY THE BOTANICALS THAT ARE INTRODUCED TO THE SPIRIT – MOST GINS USE FOUR TO SIX.

THERE ARE ESSENTIALLY THREE METHODS OF CRAFTING GIN.

COLD COMPOUNDING IS THE MOST BASIC (NOT TO MENTION THE MOST COST-EFFECTIVE!) PRODUCTION METHOD. OILS ARE EXTRACTED FROM JUNIPER & MIXED WITH A NEUTRAL SPIRIT WHICH IS THEN FILTERED & DILUTED TO BOTTLING STRENGTH.

STEEPING IS THE NEXT PROGRESSION IN THE EVOLUTION OF GIN PRODUCTION. THE BOTANICALS ARE ADDED TO THE DISTILLED SPIRIT IN THEIR NATURAL FORM AND THE MIXTURE IS BOILED. THREE THINGS INFLUENCE THE FINAL QUALITY OF THE GIN: THE BOTANICALS CHOSEN, THEIR QUALITY & FINALLY THE PERIOD OF TIME FOR WHICH THEY ARE STEEPED. STEEPING FOR A SHORT TIME PRODUCES A LIGHT-BODIED GIN. STEEP FOR A LONGER TIME & A MORE FORTHRIGHT, POWERFULLY FLAVOURED GIN IS PRODUCED. BEFORE BOTTLING THE GIN IS DILUTED, MOST COMMONLY WITH PURIFIED WATER, TO ITS REQUIRED STRENGTH.

VAPOUR INFUSION IS THE MOST SOPHISTICATED WAY OF CREATING GIN AND IS UNIQUE TO BOMBAY SAPPHIRE. A 100% GRAIN SPIRIT, TRIPLE-DISTILLED WITHIN A RARE CARTERHEAD STILL, IS PRODUCED. THE STILL REMOVES ANY IMPURITIES WITH THE RESULT THAT THE SPIRIT IS EXTREMELY PURE. THE VAPOUR RISES THROUGH A COPPER BASKET CONTAINING 10 BOTANICALS, ALLOWING EACH DELICATE FLAVOUR TO BE GENTLY ABSORBED. THE INFUSED VAPOUR SLOWLY BECOMES LIQUID AGAIN, HOLDING ALL THE BOTANICAL FLAVOURS GENTLY WITHIN. THE GIN IS THEN BLENDED WITH PURE SPRING WATER.

fire, while shades of orange and purple light glow from the fire screen and from a recess at the top of the walls. One of the walls is an illuminated sheet of glass, with white light softened and refracted by a floor-to-ceiling curtain of crystal beads, which swings away in a curve to dress the entranceway. The restaurant also features a plaster relief wall which is textured with a pattern of overlapping circles inspired by traditional Mughal masonry.

Once again the food, which is accompanied by a 100-label wine list, is delivered with a contemporary twist and seems to have curried favour with travelling gastronomes, Delhi's finest and local celebrities. All in all, it seems that Fire is cool.

Q! DIE BAR

Over the last decade hotel design has become a forum for innovation, with the social spaces – the bars, restaurants and lobbies – restoring hotels to the centre of entertainment culture. We have reached a point where we expect uniqueness in new hotel design: while the guestrooms must conjure new results from the equation of function and style, the bars and restaurants must be high-concept, exciting and different. Many attempts pale in comparison to Hotel Q! in Berlin, a truly original creation that has Q! Die Bar at its heart. It creates new territory for our relationship with space and utility, even forcing a readjustment of our expectations of walls and furniture.

London's Met Bar was the inspiration behind Q! Die Bar, which takes up most of the ground floor of the hotel. Like the Met, Q! is a hotel bar that is only open to hotel guests and members – a radical concept in London when the Met opened in 1997 and a new concept in Berlin. The restrictions give the bar privacy and exclusivity, which makes it a destination for both local and international players in the arts, film and entertainment scenes. Q! also brought on board one of the other most important elements behind the Met's initial success: Ben Reed. The former barman has become one of the world's most famous cocktail aficionados and acted as the consultant for Q!. The cocktail list includes good classics such as Black and White Russians along with some new creations. The comparisons with the Met Bar stop there, though – in design terms, Q! is in a different league. Also, its customers have none of the wannabe desperation which has begun to taint the reputation of the Met in recent years.

Q! DIE BAR, BERLIN

Q! DIE BAR
KNESEBECKSTRASSE 67,
10623 BERLIN, GERMANY

TEL +49 (0)30 810066 0
WWW.Q-BERLIN.DE

THE MIXOLOGIST: BEN REED

BEN REED FOUND FAME AT THE MET BAR IN 1997 WHEN IT WAS AT THE FOREFRONT OF LONDON'S COCKTAIL REVIVAL. HE IS NOW A BAR & COCKTAIL CONSULTANT & CREATED THE COCKTAIL LIST AT Q! DIE BAR, TAKING INTO ACCOUNT THE RADICAL DESIGN: 'YOU WANT YOUR COCKTAILS TO REFLECT THE BRAND MESSAGE OF THE BAR, IN THIS CASE, COSMOPOLITAN, MODERN, EXCLUSIVE & SOPHISTICATED.' A WELL-KNOWN WRITER ON DRINKS, WITH A REGULAR COLUMN FOR THE TIMES & SEVERAL COCKTAIL BOOKS TO HIS NAME, HE IS PART OF THE IP BARTENDERS, THE BAR & COCKTAIL CONSULTANCY WHICH IS DEDICATED TO RAISING STANDARDS. HE SAYS THAT, 'IN ALL THE BARS I HAVE RUN EMPHASIS IS ALWAYS ON THE STAFF, YOU CAN MAKE A PLACE LOOK BEAUTIFUL BUT WITHOUT GREAT STAFF IT'S JUST FOUR WALLS & A BAR.' HIS OWN FAVOURITE CREATION IS THE PURPLE HAZE, A SHOOTER MADE FROM FRESH LIME, SUGAR, VODKA, GRAND MARNIER & CHAMBORD.

The bar is a surprising red cocoon, almost entirely made up of an inner skin which bends, folds, rises and swoops to form the floor, walls, ceiling and even some of the seating. This skin is made of Marmoleum, a highly flexible relative to linoleum. It juts up from the floor to form the L-shaped bar counter, which is the pivot between the lounge and restaurant spaces, while the walls curve up from the floor and, by the side of the bar counter, curve outwards to make a bench recess. Other seating is provided by grey Little Tulip chairs by Pierre Paulin and angular divans. The restaurant area, which serves eastern Asian dishes, features semicircular booths and white drapes that can be drawn for extra privacy, while the entranceway to the lounge area is dominated by a black, monolithic, cuboid fireplace.

The bar design is established in the reception, where the similarly red flooring folds sharply upwards to create the reception desk, while the wall behind veers inwards and swoops over to form the ceiling. From the other side, this back wall forms one of the bar's unusual features, a rising series of levels and ramps which the designers Graft say, provides the option of 'walking up the walls in order to sit on top of the celebrating crowd'. This hybridisation of wall and furniture is typical of both the hotel design and Graft's whole approach. Initially based in Los Angeles, where they were hired to create a guesthouse and a studio for Brad Pitt, they now have offices in three continents, practising a desire to cross boundaries from architecture to music, art installations, car design and events.

The design of Q! is deliberately feminine in that it involves the almost complete eradication of sharp corners. The curves and folds establish a protected mini-universe – a type of womb – while the flowing nature of the design, with its unusual integration of walls and levels, simultaneously gives the freedom to step away from normal constraints. This dichotomy – a desire to be both protected and open to new possibilities – lies at the heart of successful, exclusive bar culture, which has become central to the social fabric for a new generation of style cognoscenti.

When it first opened in 2004 it seemed as if the world was going to allow Hotel Q! to slip past unnoticed, perhaps because its exterior shell reveals virtually nothing of the surprising delights that lie within, or perhaps because it is situated in West Berlin. Following the city's reunification, the former East has become the focal point for radical new architecture and the cooler elements of the entertainment scene. Its Mitte district was established as the hub for young creatives exploring new freedoms. Now that Q! is starting to get both the reputation and the awards that it undoubtedly deserves, it is reviving the kudos of the West.

BAR LODI

Situated about 20 kilometres from Milan in northern Italy, the town of Lodi has become a prime destination for style-bar lovers, even drawing the Milanese away from their own fashionable bars to seek out the pleasures of its nightlife. Bar Lodi itself is perhaps the greatest ambassador for a town that has long been linked to artistic finery through its silk, wool and majolica-ware industries. The bar was designed by Fabio Novembre back in 1998, but it still looks startlingly innovative and unique, words that are often used to describe the designer himself. Novembre, whose work includes the Shu Café and Divina club in Milan, the Una Hotel Vittoria in Florence and high-profile boutique interiors, has become one of Italy's best-known designers. Anti-corporate and highly individual, his designs are enthused by an exuberant passion to conjure new physical relationships within space. He feels that 'designers are the last defenders of the third dimension'. A long, thin, windowless corridor of just 70 metres square, the footprint for Bar Lodi is extremely unpromising, but Novembre has turned it into a theatrical adventure for cool, young urbanites.

The journey begins with an introductory capsule, a sci-fi transformation chamber that prepares the customer for a new world. With rounded corners and ovoid floor lights, the entrance space is entirely wrapped in black and white lines of varying thickness. The design, created out of Bisazza's Opus Romano mosaic tiles, is based on the barcode of Fabio Novembre's 1995 book, *A Sud di Memphis*, and has the effect of regimenting one's vision and directing the customers towards the channel running along the bar counter. The bar space is a half-tunnel with one wall,

THE DESIGNER: FABIO NOVEMBRE

'I CUT OUT SPACES IN THE VACUUM BY BLOWING AIR BUBBLES'

FABIO NOVEMBRE (BORN 1966), THE DESIGNER OF BAR LODI, HAS BECOME KNOWN FOR HIS UNIQUE & OFTEN QUITE OUTRAGEOUS DESIGNS OF BARS, RESTAURANTS, CLUBS & SHOPS, INCLUDING L'ATLANTIQUE, SHU CAFÉ & DIVINA IN MILAN. HIS MISSION, OFTEN EXPRESSED WITH A COMBINATION OF WIT, DRAMA & PHILOSOPHY, IS TO MAKE PEOPLE THINK BEYOND REDUCTIVE NORMS & EMBRACE THE POSSIBILITIES OF THEMSELVES & THEIR ENVIRONMENTS. WITH ITS LIFE-SIZE SILHOUETTES & SHADOWS, BAR LODI IS AN OBVIOUS EXPRESSION OF ONE OF THE DRIVING PRINCIPLES OF HIS DESIGNS: 'A MUTABLE THEATRE OF SHADOWS, OFFSPRING OF MYSTICAL OPACITY, IS THE CONDITION I TRY TO CREATE IN MY WORK.'

decorated with variations of brown Bisazza tiles, curving over to form the ceiling. A gap has been sliced horizontally through this wall to create the bar counter. At a distance, the pixelation of the tiny tiles makes the curving wall look like granite. As well as adding drama to the space, the curve up to the ceiling cleverly hides the air-conditioning system: Novembre may be associated with grand design effects but he often incorporates a more utilitarian capacity for problem-solving.

The opposing wall is a sheer plane of mirrors, which helps solve the dimensional difficulties of the narrow space but also creates the bar's primary coup de théâtre. Using the figures in Richard Avedon's famous 1969 photographic portrait of Andy Warhol and members of the Factory, Novembre has removed the silver from the back of the mirror panels to create life-size silhouettes along the length of the bar. White fluorescent light is shone through the silhouettes to form the bar's main light source. A unique aesthetic, stylistic historical resonance and logistics are combined in a single, arresting solution. The shadows of the silhouettes are cast across the floor, picked out in dark mosaic tiles. The

main bar space is too narrow to incorporate furniture alongside the bar counter, and the standing demeanour of these ever-present, life-size ghosts makes it seem more natural to stand. Novembre says, 'All this, besides solving the lighting needs, gives the sense of presence of people even when the bar is empty.' The bar's enduring popularity ensures that is unlikely to be empty, but these figures, drawn from such a cool, iconic and creative assemblage as the Factory, add to the sense that the creative, cutting-edge customers of Bar Lodi are in like-minded company.

At the end of the tunnel, the space opens up slightly once more. The design of the entranceway, with the bar-code mosaic wrapping around the walls, is repeated, but mirror panels are used on some of the wall surfaces in order to extend the barcode effect. This end point houses the only furniture in Bar Lodi. The two-tiered Amat tables are in polished aluminium, with a textured top surface which fractures light and corresponds to the surrounding mosaic, while the Costantino white-and-silver stools are designed by Carlo Mollino.

IN THE MIX: VERMOUTH

VERMOUTH IS PROBABLY AN ITALIAN INVENTION LIKELY TO DATE FROM THE EARLY 18TH CENTURY, BUT THE WORD IS DERIVED FROM *WERMUT*, THE GERMAN FOR WORMWOOD. ALL VERMOUTH, WHETHER RED, WHITE OR DRY IS WINE INFUSED WITH HERBS & OTHER BOTANICALS & THE GERMANS OFTEN USED WORMWOOD TO AROMATIZE THEIR WINES. WHEREVER IT FIRST STARTED, ITALIANS BECAME THE GREAT VERMOUTH CONSUMERS & THE BRAND MARTINI & ROSSI IS THE MOST FAMOUS VERMOUTH WORLDWIDE, HELPED NO DOUBT BY THE NAME MARTINI BEING USED TO DESCRIBE THE ULTIMATE, CLASSIC COCKTAIL. THE FIRST MARTINI BRAND WAS THE SWEET, ROSSO VERSION, WHICH GETS ITS COLOUR FROM TRADITIONAL CARAMEL. PRODUCTION BEGAN IN 1863, WITH EXTRA DRY LAUNCHED ON NEW YEAR'S DAY 1900 & BIANCO A DECADE LATER. ALL THREE TYPES OF VERMOUTH HAVE BECOME STAPLES OF COCKTAIL CULTURE, BOTH OLD & NEW, WITH SOME COCKTAILS SUCH AS THE BRONX REQUIRING MORE THAN ONE VARIETY.

THE BRONX

INGREDIENTS:
30 ML (1 OZ) GIN
25 ML (0.75 OZ) DRY VERMOUTH
25 ML (0.75 OZ) SWEET VERMOUTH
50ML (1.5 OZ) FRESH ORANGE
JUICE

METHOD:
SHAKE WITH ICE & STRAIN
GLASS: MARTINI
GARNISH: NONE

EAST

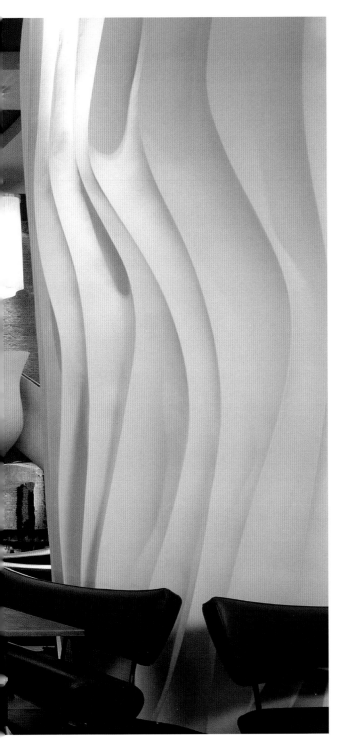

East Restaurant and its bars are just about incomparable to any other establishment, largely because of the very distinctive style of Jordan Mozer and Associates (JMA), a Chicago-based design company. With its cathedral-like proportions, and huge, mushroom-stalk pillars, the nearest reference point for East – aside from the designer's own previous work – is probably the work of Antonio Gaudí, with whom Mozer seems to share a passion for both organic forms and unbridled nonconformity. Any further comparison to Gaudí would be to head down a blind alley, though. Mozer is a true original who has found success in the architectural genres where aesthetic risk and innovation are now most likely to be prevalent: bars, restaurants and hotels.

East emerged from the ruins of an abandoned old iron foundry in Hamburg in 2005. It's a 250-cover Asian-fusion restaurant, with influences ranging from India to Japan, that has four bar spaces and a boutique hotel attached, with most of the guestrooms set in a new purpose-built block. This addition gave rise to the opportunity to create a garden courtyard between the two buildings. The old and new buildings together form a doughnut, as Mozer describes it, with the garden courtyard in the middle. The old foundry section has also been modelled as a doughnut ('a doughnut within a doughnut'), with the grand, 12-metre high main restaurant space as the 'hole' or interior courtyard. More intimate dining and bar spaces are set around the restaurant courtyard's three-storey-high walls. The influences on the design are multifarious, ranging from the magical realism of Gabriel Garcia Márquez to the colours and shapes of Asian design, while also drawing on the building's former use as a foundry.

The restaurant is a tremendous space with white, carved plasterwork pillars giving the design a monumental aspect which is further emphasised by a three-storey plasterwork wall – called the 'Hive' – with angled contours of plaster surrounding cut out, internal windows. It may draw inspiration from beehives, but it looks like a surrealist rendition of a cliff of hermit caves. The pillars reach up to a grid-patterned ceiling featuring spun aluminium chandeliers hung with sheer white fabric. One side of the restaurant is dominated by four 28-foot-high glass doors leading out to the garden courtyard. Sections of brickwork amongst the white plaster, along with smoked-oak parquet flooring and oak tables, temper the otherworldliness of the space. Most of the interior design features of East have been specially created by JMA in tandem with various artists and manufacturers. The restaurant has very distinctive chair designs made from a colour-integrated, fibreglass-and-Kevlar-reinforced resin, which has been hand-finished to create a satin sheen. Inspired by the building's former use as an iron foundry, certain elements have been made from cast materials, including three-legged tables and bar stools which are cast from an aluminium–magnesium alloy.

Access to East is through a double-height entranceway which leads to a choice of two bars: the Lobby Bar and Yakshi's Bar which overlooks the interior courtyard from one side. There is also a terrace for views over the garden courtyard. The old, chipped brickwork of the foundry has been left rawly exposed throughout the two bars but is augmented by sculptural white plasterwork. The Lobby Bar features a broad counter-table which forms the base of

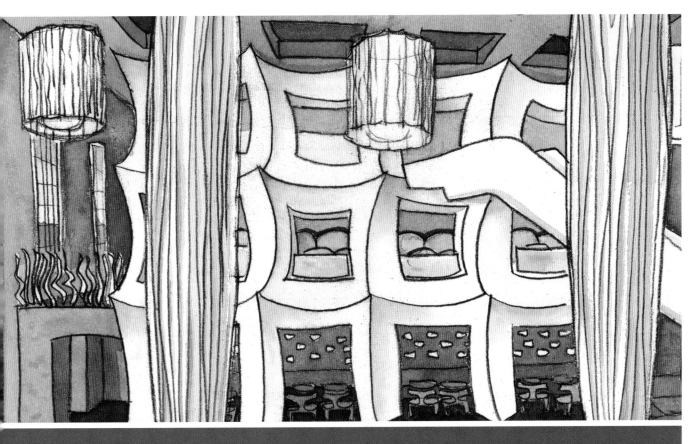

THE DESIGNER:
JORDAN MOZER

JORDAN MOZER FOUNDED JORDAN MOZER & ASSOCIATES IN 1984 & SAYS THAT HE CAME TO BE ASKED TO DESIGN EAST IN HAMBURG BECAUSE OF A PIG. IN 1990 HE WAS COMMISSIONED TO DESIGN THE CYPRESS CLUB RESTAURANT IN SAN FRANCISCO & REALISED HE'D FOUND THE PERFECT DESIGN SOLUTION WHEN HE WAS SKETCHING HIS PET PIG. THE DESIGN OF THE CYPRESS CLUB, WITH ITS FAT, ORGANIC SHAPES, WAS A HUGE HIT & JMA HAS GONE ON TO SCORE SUCCESSES WITH MORE RESTAURANTS INCLUDING THE HUDSON CLUB & THE CHEESECAKE FACTORY IN CHICAGO & HERZBLUT IN HAMBURG. EAST COMBINES JMA'S SIGNATURE CURVES & ORGANIC SHAPES WITH A TASTE FOR MAGICAL REALISM & MORE LOCALISED INFLUENCES SUCH AS THE RESTAURANT'S EASTERN-INSPIRED CUISINE & THE BUILDING'S FORMER LIFE AS AN IRON FOUNDRY: 'CAST ELEMENTS SUGGEST FORMS FOUND IN NATURE. WESTERN STORIES OFTEN INVOLVE CONFLICT BETWEEN MAN & NATURE; SOME EASTERN THOUGHT RECOGNISES SPIRITUAL PERFECTION IN THE FORMS OF NATURE. '

EAST, HAMBURG

EAST
SIMON-VON-UTRECHT-STRASSE 31,
20359 HAMBURG, GERMANY
TEL +49 (0)40 30 99 30

WWW.EAST-HAMBURG.DE
OR WWW.DESIGNHOTELS.COM

IN THE MIX: VODKA

BOTH RUSSIA & POLAND CLAIM THE INVENTION OF VODKA, WHICH FIRST EMERGED IN AROUND THE 12TH CENTURY, & BOTH COUNTRIES CONTINUE TO HAVE A HUGE AMOUNT OF PRIDE IN THEIR QUALITY VODKA PRODUCTION. LIKE MOST SPIRITS, IT BEGAN LIFE AS A MEDICINAL CONCOCTION BUT IN RUSSIA IT EVEN TOOK ON RELIGIOUS SIGNIFICANCE & WAS CONSUMED COMMUNALLY ON SIGNIFICANT HOLY DAYS. POTATOES WERE USUALLY THE PRIME INGREDIENT BUT VODKA IS NOW LARGELY A GRAIN-BASED SPIRIT. THE EARLY DAYS OF COCKTAIL CULTURE WERE A VODKA-FREE ZONE (VODKA WASN'T COMMON IN THE US AT ALL UNTIL THE 1930S) BUT THE LATE 20TH CENTURY SAW A HUGE REVIVAL IN ITS FORTUNES. THIS IS SOMETIMES PUT DOWN TO THE FACT THAT IT CAN BE EASILY MASKED BY OTHER FLAVOURS & IS THEREFORE THE FIRST PORT OF CALL FOR AN UNSOPHISTICATED PALATE. HOWEVER, IN RECENT YEARS, WITH THE RAPIDLY GROWING DISCERNMENT OF COCKTAIL DRINKERS WORLDWIDE, LEADING MIXOLOGISTS HAVE EMPHASISED THE DISTINCTIVE FLAVOURS OF PREMIUM VODKAS SUCH AS GREY GOOSE & THE VERY BEST POLISH & RUSSIAN BRANDS.

GREY GOOSE LE CITRON
LEMON DROP MARTINI

INGREDIENTS:
50 ML (1.5 OZ) GREY GOOSE LE CITRON VODKA
1 LEMON
SUGAR

METHOD:
ADD VODKA & A SQUEEZE OF LEMON TO AN ICE-FILLED SHAKER, SHAKE & STRAIN INTO A SUGAR-RIMMED GLASS
GLASS: MARTINI
GARNISH: LEMON TWIST

a hole cut into an angled white wall and is decorated with snaking, red-bronze candlesticks, copper bowls filled with spices, and blown-glass pendant drops. East's Asian-fusion menu is complemented by an immense choice of cocktails at Yakshi's, which has a long wooden counter and high wooden tables, all in oak, and introduces the restaurant's theme of sculpted, organic pillars. The Asian influence has been conscientiously explored in drinks such as the Tamarino, a mix of gin, tamarind and lime juice, and the Frozen Frog which blends Midori, *pisang ambong*, *kwai feh* and lime juice.

Through the Hive windows on the other side of the courtyard from Yakshi's, one can see the pink glow of the Colours Lounge, another unique bar space which is filled with red beanbag seating. One side of the lounge is dominated by Mozer's sculptural artwork, called *Dancing Yin Yang*, of yellow, bulbous, interlocking forms that are inspired by bi-electron microscope photographs. The Lounge also has an exterior terrace overlooking a garden courtyard. Hamburg is increasingly becoming known as a design lover's city, and East is its most adventurous jewel.

With Hakkasan and its Ling Ling lounge continuing to buzz all week long, stuffed to the gills with celebrities and style gurus ever since its 2001 opening, it's difficult to remember what a risk it was for restaurateur Alan Yau. He made his name with Wagamama, which has become an international chain of around 50 restaurants since 1992 when it first surprised Londoners with its blend of cool design, communal tables and cheap noodles, in Bloomsbury. People have a great affection for Wagamama, despite the fact that it's a chain, and it was even crowned as Zagat's 'Most Popular' London eatery in 2006, pushing the likes of Nobu and Gordon Ramsay's restaurants down the list. The key to Wagamama's success is its sleek, minimalist design originally conceived by John Pawson: the food may be cheap, but the customers don't feel sullied by their association with what has become a mass-market outlet. However, customer expectations at the high end of the restaurant scene are completely different. The success of Hakkasan revealed that Yau really does possess the golden touch. In 2003, it won a much coveted Michelin star, an extraordinary first for a British restaurant specialising in Chinese food, a cuisine which does not usually appeal to the rarefied tastes of the Michelin judges.

Hakkasan's menu is largely influenced by various regions of China but the name itself reveals wider, pan-Asian traits. Hakka is a Chinese ethnic group that grew up around the Yellow River, and *san* is a Japanese title of respect that is added to a person's name. During the day, the restaurant specialises in innovative dim sum, establishing new taste adventures within the Chinese tradition of small dishes, with an à

THE DESIGNER:
CHRISTIAN LIAIGRE

THE DESIGNER OF HAKKASAN, CHRISTIAN LIAIGRE, IS FAMOUS FOR BOTH HIS INTERIORS & HIS FURNITURE DESIGNS WHICH ARE OFTEN UNITED BY A REJECTION OF SUPERFLUOUS DECORATION. BORN IN LA ROCHELLE, FRANCE, HE IS A FAVOURITE WITH FASHION DESIGNERS, CREATING THE HOMES OF CALVIN KLEIN & KARL LAGERFELD, & DESIGNED THE INTERIORS FOR RUPERT MURDOCH'S NEW YORK RESIDENCE. OTHER DESIGNS INCLUDE THE MARKET RESTAURANT IN PARIS, THE MERCER HOTEL IN NEW YORK, WHICH HAS BEEN THE FASHIONISTAS' NEW YORK NEST OF CHOICE SINCE 1997, & THE RESTAURANT FOR MADRID'S HOTEL PUERTA AMÉRICA ALL-STAR DESIGN PROJECT. BEFORE DESIGNING HAKKASAN, LIAIGRE HAD ALREADY SHOWN HIS SKILL AT MERGING EASTERN & WESTERN INFLUENCES WITH WORK IN THAILAND & IN HIS DESIGNS FOR THE SHOZAN RESTAURANT IN PARIS. LIAIGRE WORKED WITH ALAN YAU AGAIN FOR YAUATCHA, HAKKASAN'S SISTER RESTAURANT WHICH OPENED IN LONDON IN 2004.

la carte menu in the evenings. The main restaurant is accompanied by Ling Ling, a more informal lounge and bar which offers the same cuisine and has become a destination for oriental-influenced cocktails which are becoming increasingly popular.

In order to establish Hakkasan as a unique, high-calibre restaurant that is very different from Wagamama, innovative design played as important a part as the adventurous menu. Yau stepped away from the purely minimalist ethos that had brought success to his chain and hired Christian Liaigre to create a dark, sultry, fashionable restaurant which would have both finesse and mystery while drawing upon Chinese tradition. Liaigre is famous for designing the homes of celebrities, particularly from the world of haute couture. The intention was clear: Hakkasan was to be bespoke. Yau wanted Liaigre to design the interior with a view to 'bringing back the dragon', contrasting with the clinical simplicity which has come to dominate designs of contemporary East Asian restaurants in the West. The result is the absorption of the signposts of Chinese culture – the screens, lanterns, latticework and ornate, detailed imagery – into an ultramodern design.

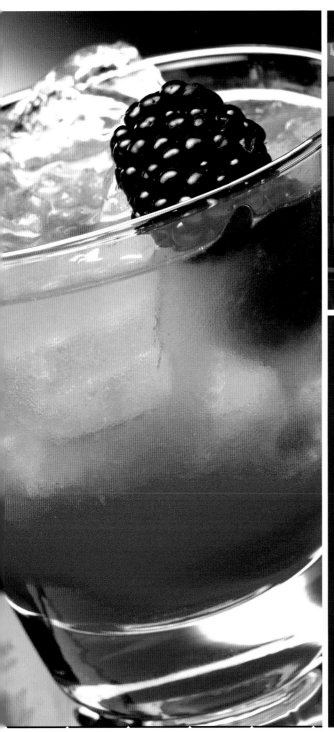

CLASSIC COCKTAILS:
THE BOMBAY BRAMBLE

OVER THE LAST DECADE OR SO, A NEW BREED OF CLASSIC COCKTAIL HAS EMERGED. EVEN THOUGH THEY ARE RECENT CREATIONS, DRINKS SUCH AS THE APPLE MARTINI & THE SAKETINI HAVE BECOME STAPLES OF COCKTAIL MENUS ALL OVER THE WORLD. ONE OF THE MOST POPULAR 'NEW CLASSICS' IS THE BOMBAY BRAMBLE WHICH BALANCES THE FRUITINESS OF FRESH BLACKBERRIES, THE SHARPNESS OF LEMON JUICE & THE SMOOTHNESS OF A SUBTLE, COMPLEX GIN FOR AN ALL-YEAR-ROUND FAVOURITE.

INGREDIENTS:
30 ML (1 OZ) BOMBAY SAPPHIRE GIN
25 ML (0.75 OZ) FRESH LEMON JUICE
DASH OF SUGAR SYRUP TO TASTE
FLOAT OF CRÈME DE MURE

METHOD:
POUR THE FIRST 3 INGREDIENTS INTO A ROCKS GLASS FILLED WITH CRUSHED ICE & THEN GENTLY STIR. FLOAT THE CRÈME DE MURE OVER THE TOP OF THE DRINK
GLASS: ROCKS
GARNISH: SINGLE BLACKBERRY OR A SLICE OF LEMON

HAKKASAN, LONDON

HAKKASAN
8 HANWAY PLACE,
LONDON W1T 1HF

TEL +44 (0)20 7927 7000

The tables and surrounding screens are made of dark-stained English oak which gives a graceful solidity to the restaurant. The main dining area and the bar, which is a strip of stools along a 16-metre counter also in stained oak, are divided by a huge lattice screen. This has been cut into a great variety of geometrical patterns that allow glimpses of the adjacent spaces. Above the bar counter is a wall of rough slate, adding a fractured texture to the décor, which otherwise relies on a rather smooth linearity. Surrounding the dining area, blue glass is used within backlit panels and latticework to create an interesting light-box effect. The lighting is the work of Arnold Chan, one of the world's leading lighting designers, who created the famous kaleidoscope effect of St Martin's Lane Hotel. Blue is used again for the leather seating and panels of Ling Ling, which also has low, white marble tables. The backs of the armchairs are decorated with red, gold and blue Chinese artworks, marrying the über-cool lounge setting with traditional influences. Chinese-lantern-design and antique lacquered panels are skilfully integrated and reinterpreted throughout the restaurant. Combined with the unusual pairings of flavours in both the food and drink menus, the overall effect is to create a glamorous, inspiring but relaxed ambience.

Following the opening of Hakkasan, Alan Yau was awarded the 2002 London Restaurant Award for 'Outstanding Contribution', while the restaurant has also won countless other best oriental restaurant, best newcomer and best restaurant design awards.

BAR STRAF

If there's any city where a combination of exclusive bar style and Brutalist design can be pulled off, it is Milan. The rawness of Brutalism particularly reverberates with a city known for combining the opposing attractions of haute couture and heavy industry, and Milan houses some prime examples of Brutalist-influenced architecture including Gio Ponti's Pirelli Building and Vittoriano Viganò's Istituto Marchiondi. The Milanese are perhaps the most fashionable people in the world, but growing up in a city choking with factories, they are not averse to mixing a little gritty functionalism with their aesthetics. Bar Straf, a daringly Brutalist bar right in the centre of Milan, has become a favourite with the shades-wearing locals attracted to a design full of distressed or scratched textures and featuring iron, concrete, slate, glass and brass.

Brutalism, which comes from the term béton brut (raw concrete), can be seen as a sort of anti-aesthetic where the 'truth' of the building materials and the building process itself remains part of the finished design. As a result, surfaces can seem unfinished or distressed while the usually hidden structure and services of the building are exposed. It is an unlikely starting point for a bar that trades on cocktail culture, a genre usually associated with luxury materials, veneers and polish. But Brutalism is not just functional. It may have its roots in a modernist sense of geometry, but the best buildings in the style often involve a monumental irregularity – a unique, surprising and heroic design feature which can make a

IN THE MIX: ITALIAN COCKTAILS

ITALY HAS A GREAT FAMILY TRADITION OF THE *APERITIVO*, ITS OWN VERSION OF THE COCKTAIL HOUR, & HAS CONTRIBUTED A GREAT AMOUNT TO THE INGREDIENTS USED IN COCKTAILS WORLDWIDE. VERMOUTH, THE HERB-INFUSED WINE, ORIGINATED IN ITALY AT AROUND THE BEGINNING OF THE 18TH CENTURY, WITH THE WORLD-FAMOUS MARTINI & ROSSI BRAND STARTING PRODUCTION IN 1863. CAMPARI, AN INFUSION OF HERBS, PLANTS & FRUIT, WAS INVENTED IN 1860 & WENT ON TO BECOME A STANDARD INGREDIENT OF THE NEGRONI & THE AMERICANO AS WELL AS OFTEN BEING DRUNK WITH SODA. DISARONNO AMARETTO, THE BIGGEST-SELLING ITALIAN LIQUEUR, IS ALSO BEING USED TO CREATE INTERESTING COCKTAIL VARIATIONS. CONTRARY TO POPULAR BELIEF, IT IS NOT MADE FROM ALMONDS BUT CONTAINS ALCOHOL, BURNT SUGAR & 17 HERBS & FRUITS SOAKED IN APRICOT KERNEL OIL.

AMARETTO SOUR

INGREDIENTS:	METHOD:
50 ML (1.5 OZ) AMARETTO	SHAKE WITH ICE & STRAIN
15 ML (0.5 OZ) LEMON JUICE	**GLASS:** SOUR GLASS
DASH OF BITTERS	**GARNISH:** ORANGE SLICE

building loved and loathed in equal measure (the Barbican Centre and Trelleck Tower in London are great examples). In the end, anti-aestheticism has its own aesthetic appeal: the cool young Milanese who love Bar Straf also understand that half the passers-by who peer through its glazed exterior will just not 'get it', and that makes it all the more attractive. Inside, it is relaxed rather than overly modish, managing to combine the comfortable with the unconventional to good effect. Oddly, the result of its panels of distressed materials, which have been combined with antique furnishings, is quite baroque.

The bar is connected to Hotel Straf but, with an on-street entrance, it works as an independent entity for people popping in all day for a late breakfast, an after-shopping aperitif or night-time drink. Straf's name is an abbreviation of its address on the Via San Raffaele, a location that couldn't be much more ideal as it's a quiet street situated in the golden quadrangle district of fashion boutiques and close to both the Duomo and La Scala. The hotel and the bar, which opened in 2004, are designed by Vincenzo de Cotiis, an architect who is also famous as a fashion designer. His couture includes the Haute Collection and is typified by reclaimed vintage materials that have been reinvented within a contemporary context.

BAR STRAF, MILAN

BAR STRAF
VIA SAN RAFFAELE 3,
MILAN 20121,
ITALY

TEL +39 02 805 081
WWW.STRAF.IT OR WWW.DESIGNHOTELS.COM

EQUIPPED WITH STYLE:
870 COCKTAIL SHAKER BY
LUIGI MASSONI AND CARLO MAZZERI

ONE OF THE FIRST PRODUCTS CREATED BY ITALIAN DESIGNERS LUIGI MASSONI &
CARLO MAZZERI WAS THEIR 1957 COCKTAIL SHAKER, WHICH WAS ALSO ONE OF THE
VERY FIRST ALESSI OBJECTS DEVISED BY EXTERNAL DESIGNERS. MADE FROM MATT
STAINLESS STEEL, IT IS STILL IN PRODUCTION ALMOST 50 YEARS LATER & HAS BECOME
AN ALESSI CLASSIC COMMONLY USED BY PROFESSIONAL MIXOLOGISTS. MILAN-BORN
MASSONI WENT ON TO DESIGN FOR BOFFI, CREATING SOME OF THE FIRST MODULAR
DESIGNS FOR THE HOME, WHILE MAZZERI TEAMED UP WITH ANSELMO VITALE TO
DEVELOP ALESSI'S HUGE RANGE OF AVIO PRODUCTS.

This same methodology has been used for Bar Straf. Within the shell of unpainted concrete and glass, there is a myriad of nonfigurative artworks that together create a patchwork of textures, colours and reclaimed materials. Vintage red-leather and wooden stools line the bar and the side shelving while the rest of the furniture includes a beaten-up brown-leather sofa forming an L-shape, modern black-leather cubic pouffes, and a burnished table. An unadorned, scarred Doric column – revealing the building's origins as a 19th-century palazzo – stands in the middle of the room, right against the all-black, ardently minimalist bar counter and glass display. The unusual proximity and contrast of the counter and pillar are effective in creating a sense of unconventionality. The hotel guests and the local patrons seem to mix well, which is little surprise as both seem to consist mainly of models, artists, photographers and stylish businesspeople. The photographers are, perhaps, drawn to the restrooms, where the walls are decorated entirely with huge photographic murals of the human form (at the athletic end of the spectrum). The hotel also has an additional room for breakfast and lunch. This is a more purely minimalist creation, again cased in raw concrete but featuring strictly cubic furniture, entirely in black and white.

SETAI

Even the A-list celebrities sipping cocktails by the pool of the Delano or lounging in the Red Room of the Shore Club may be wondering where some of the beautiful people have gone. Miami's South Beach, which has long been the heart of the best of the city's architecture and nightlife, has a new contender for hippest place on the planet – the Setai – which has managed to ramp up the global fascination with the city's celebrity-laden hotel culture to even greater extremes. As with Miami's other great hotels, the Setai's success is found in coupling South Beach's Art Deco heritage and shore-side location with topnotch restaurants and bars. The hotel opened in 2004 but the Setai really took off with the 2005 completion of its restaurant and the Champagne Crustacean and Caviar Bar, joining its graceful lobby bar and outside pool bar (de rigueur for any South Beach venture worth its salt).

The Setai is an exact replica of the Vanderbilt Hotel which formerly stood on the site. An Art Deco landmark completed in 1938, the eight-storey building was owned by legendary boxer Jack Dempsey and it became an iconic celebrity hangout (these days even an original Dempsey-Vanderbilt swizzle stick will set collectors back $75). The new building is owned by a more modern legend, hotelier Adrian Zecha, whose GHM Hotels manage many of Asia's best resorts. He also runs the successful T8 restaurant and bar in Shanghai, a city's whose own Art Deco heritage helped inspire the newly originated interior of the Setai.

Inside, the hotel is Eastern-orientated in both ethos and aesthetic. The lobby, bar and restaurants are decorated with dark-grey bricks

reclaimed from derelict Art Deco buildings in Shanghai and, throughout, the design is augmented by traditional East Asian materials such as teak and bronze as well as Asian artworks and objects. The bar stretches from the lobby towards the courtyard and features a row of long tube lights aligned like organ pipes above the sleek counter. The dark wood of the intricate, latticework panels behind the bar counter is offset by the luminous, shattered rainbow of the mother-of-pearl counter-top. The Setai's latticework designs are made from Burmese teak but are inspired by Art Deco patterns from Belgium, emphasising the fusion of American, Asian and European influences that inspire the individuality of the Setai's design and its cuisine.

The bar is the place for cocktails and single malt whiskies, but wine aficionados should head into the Champagne Crustacean and Caviar Bar, which perhaps could benefit from a name which isn't quite such a literally descriptive mouthful. The design also features the Chinese brickwork along with a dark ceiling textured with interweaving ribbons of teak. Floor-to-ceiling cabinets show off the very extensive wine collection but cocktail lovers are still catered for, with the mixologists creating giant, $100 dollar cocktails for four to share. Large oriental pots and statues add to the exotic, sophisticated mood while glazed doors lead onto one of the hotel's other delights: the courtyard.

COCKTAIL CONNECTIONS: ERNEST HEMINGWAY

THE LEGENDARY AMERICAN WRITER ERNEST HEMINGWAY (1899–1961), AUTHOR OF *FOR WHOM THE BELL TOLLS*, WILL ALWAYS BE ASSOCIATED WITH BARS HE FREQUENTED ACROSS THE GLOBE, BUT CLOSER TO HOME, HE WAS A MEMBER OF THE KEY WEST MOB WHO CAROUSED IN THE BARS OF FLORIDA. HEMINGWAY LIVED IN KEY WEST FOR A DECADE & IMMORTALISED ONE OF THE MOB, JOE RUSSELL, IN HIS 1937 NOVEL *TO HAVE AND HAVE NOT* ABOUT A BOOTLEG RUM-RUNNER. RUSSELL, WHO WAS PLAYED BY HUMPHREY BOGART IN THE FILM VERSION, OWNED SLOPPY JOE'S BAR WHERE HEMINGWAY DOWNED MANY A DAIQUIRI. IN THE LARGELY AUTOBIOGRAPHICAL NOVEL *ISLANDS IN THE STREAM*, HEMINGWAY WROTE THAT DRINKING A DAIQUIRI FELT 'THE WAY DOWNHILL GLACIER SKIING FEELS RUNNING THROUGH POWDER SNOW AND, AFTER THE SIXTH & EIGHT, FELT LIKE DOWNHILL GLACIER SKIING FEELS WHEN YOU ARE RUNNING UNROPED.'

DAIQUIRI

INGREDIENTS:
50 ML (1.5 OZ) BACARDI WHITE RUM
30 ML (1 OZ) FRESH LIME JUICE
DASH OF SUGAR SYRUP TO TASTE

METHOD:
SHAKE WITH ICE & STRAIN
GLASS: MARTINI
GARNISH: NONE

SETAI, MIAMI

SETAI
2001 COLLINS AVENUE,
MIAMI, FLORIDA 33139,
USA

TEL +1 305 520 6000
WWW.SETAI.COM

CLASSIC COCKTAILS: THE MOJITO

ONE OF THE 'NEW CLASSICS' OF THE CONTEMPORARY COCKTAIL AGE, FEATURING ON ALMOST EVERY EXTENSIVE COCKTAIL LIST, IS THE MOJITO WHICH HAS TAKEN OVER FROM DAIQUIRI AS A HUGELY POPULAR RUM COCKTAIL. IT HAS THE SAME BASE INGREDIENTS BUT ADDS FRESH MINT LEAVES & SODA. A FEATURE OF CUBAN LIFE FOR MORE THAN A CENTURY, ITS GLOBAL RENAISSANCE IS PARTLY DOWN TO THE MIAMI BAR SCENE WHICH HOTELS SUCH AS THE DELANO, THE SHORE CLUB, THE VICTOR & NOW THE SETAI HAVE HELPED TO REVIVE.

INGREDIENTS:
50 ML (1.5 OZ) BACARDI WHITE RUM
12 MINT LEAVES
1/2 FRESH LIME
2 TBSP SUGAR
SODA

METHOD:
MUDDLE THE MINT & LIME IN THE BOTTOM OF THE GLASS, ADD SUGAR & FILL WITH ICE. POUR IN RUM & SODA AND GENTLY STIR
GLASS: HIGHBALL
GARNISH: MINT LEAVES & SLICE OF LIME

The main restaurant won *Esquire* magazine's Best Designed Restaurant 2005, which seems sure to be joined by further awards in the coming years. The lobby, bars and restaurant are a transglobal collaboration between Belgian-born architect Jean-Michel Gathy of Denniston International, Jaya Ibrahim & Associates of Jakarta and Spin Studio of Japan, while the cuisine is given a further international twist by Australian head chef Shaun Danyel Hergatt. Brought to Miami from the Atelier at the New York Ritz-Carlton, he has created an Asian and French-influenced menu with an emphasis on fresh produce. The flooring is a pleasing geometric pattern made of leather panels bordered by tropical hardwood, while the combination of dark brick, panelling and

furniture ensure a dark and moody setting. However, one of the restaurant's showpieces is its stainless-steel exhibition kitchen, which gives the restaurant a continual, natural buzz.

As is usual for one of South Beach's stellar hot spots, a good part of the action is outside. The courtyard features tables, set in a series of sunken pods amongst the tall pergolas, for both diners and drinkers. The Setai's 90-foot Pool Bar is another impressive feature, with its centrepiece looking like an Art Deco temple overseeing the parade of three pools, each with a different water temperature.

Mourad 'Momo' Mazouz, the Algerian son of Berbers, and business partner David Ponte wandered around London on a motorbike for two years looking for a site for a new restaurant. When Momo opened in 1997, it turned the quiet but central Heddon Street into an epicentre for Maghrebi culture. Madonna et al flocked through its doors and it remains a celebrity haven. For hundreds of years, Maghrebi culture – which is often just called Moroccan but originates from Morocco, Algeria and Tunisia – has been enthused by a love for luscious and intense colours, textures, flavours and fragrances. Its designs have long been incorporated into European culture but have found a new worldwide influence in the last decade. Momo's impact has been deeply felt, influencing British design and helping to incorporate a greater taste for fresh, exotic and intense flavours into the mainstream. Created by Mazouz alongside Fusion and The Design Consultancy, the Momo enterprise now includes the downstairs Kemia bar, which has become London's prime venue for North African and Arabian music, and the Mo Tearoom & Bazaar, a *shisha*-smoking, tea-drinking, cocktail lover's paradise.

Tall brass candlesticks and arched wooden doors lead the way into the main restaurant, where elements of the souk are found in the display of spices and piles of baskets, plates and tagines around an old-fashioned, Arabic-inscribed weighing scale. However, the restaurant design is serene and luxurious, and far removed from the chaos of a market. North African style abounds, with Arabian carpets, intricate white

COCKTAIL CONNECTIONS: CASABLANCA

'OF ALL THE GIN JOINTS IN ALL THE TOWNS IN ALL OF THE WORLD, SHE WALKS INTO MINE.'

RICK'S, PROBABLY THE MOST FAMOUS BAR IN FILM HISTORY, IS THE FOCUS FOR SO MUCH OF *CASABLANCA* (1942) THAT ITS ORIGINAL TITLE WAS 'EVERYBODY COMES TO RICK'S'. THE DOOMED LOVE STORY BETWEEN HUMPHREY BOGART & INGRID BERGMAN WAS HEIGHTENED BY THE EXOTIC MOROCCAN SETTING, WITH RICK'S HELPING TO SET THE MOOD WITH CARVED WOODEN SCREENS, LANTERNS, TASSELS & TILES. THERE'S A RASH OF FAUX RICK'S BARS ACROSS THE WORLD BUT, FORTUNATELY, THE RISE OF THE MAGHREBI CULTURAL INFLUENCE MEANS THAT PUNTERS DON'T HAVE TO LOOK TOO FAR TO ENJOY THE GENUINE NORTH AFRICAN ARTICLE.

plasterwork and carved wooden screens. The room's centrepiece is a large, exotic lantern, hanging from a shallow dome, which gives the room a relaxing amber tone. The patrons sit on the terracotta-coloured leather cushions of miniature, carved wooden chairs, choosing from classic and contemporary Maghrebi dishes flavoured with harissa and coriander oil, and drink cocktails such as the Momo Special, a blend of vodka, lemon, *gomme*, soda and a whole herb garden's worth of fresh mint. Cocktails like the Bombay Bellini and Pommery-topped Marrakech o Marrakech are also the order of the day at the elite Kemia bar which evokes a Moorish tent with a melange of low sofas and exotic cushions. The plush space acts as a live music venue on Mondays and Tuesdays, and a private members' DJ bar for the rest of the week. As ever, Momo's influence spreads wide – Kemia is the inspiration for a range of successful chill-out records, including Arabesque 1, 2 and 3 and Africanesque.

If the restaurant is a soft, stately introduction to Maghrebi style, the tearoom is a full-on souk. Its wooden ceiling is bedecked with dozens of bronze, copper and brass lanterns, shimmering with coloured glass and pendants, which are for sale. Upright, carved wooden corner seats accompany a six-sided table featuring mother-

MOMO, LONDON

MOMO
25 HEDDON STREET,
LONDON W1B 4BH, UK

TEL +44 (0)20 7434 4040

INSPIRED CREATIONS:
MAGHREBI SAPPHIRE BY JAMIE WALKER

INGREDIENTS:
50 ML (1.5 OZ) BOMBAY SAPPHIRE GIN
25 ML (0.75 OZ) GINGER
LEMON CORDIAL
15-20 LEAVES OF MINT
CINNAMON
SODA

METHOD:
MUDDLE THE MINT & A SPRINKLE OF
CINNAMON IN A BOSTON SHAKER, ADD
BOMBAY SAPPHIRE, THE GINGER &
LEMON CORDIAL & ICE. SHAKE, POUR
& TOP WITH SODA.
GLASS: HIGHBALL
GARNISH: MINT

of-pearl marquetry, while the other seating is made up of hide-covered pouffes and cushion-laden benches surrounding brass-tray-topped tables. With a casual but stylish clientele smoking fruit-flavoured *shishas* and drinking exotic cocktails and teas, it's a sensual oasis in which the importance of time and the chaotic crush of London are easily forgotten.

Mazouz has gone on to create Sketch, the high-design, art-inspired restaurant, gallery and bar complex, but his personality still courses through this evolving, and ever-popular, Maghrebi journey of the senses. Since Momo opened, there has been a greater understanding of the depth of North African culture, and the cuisine is no longer confused with the output of a dodgy kebab shop. Sam and Sam Clark have brought further recognition of the culinary delights of the region through Moro, another hugely successful London restaurant, while both Momo and Moro have produced huge-selling cookbooks. Ten years ago, no one could have foreseen that the houses of Acacia Avenue would be filled with the heady scents of the Maghreb.

BLOWFISH
RESTAURANT
& SAKÉ BAR

Blowfish Restaurant & Saké Bar is the chicest place in Toronto, which is no mean feat in a city increasingly crammed with extremely well-designed bars and restaurants. Its citizens, whose civic pride is the most intense you are ever likely to encounter, are fed up with having Toronto besmirched with descriptions such as 'sedate' and 'provincial', epithets that no longer suit this Ontario city that exploded into life in the late 20th century. Recently, a rigorous scientific formula was applied to find out the place in the world that had the highest quality of living, and the answer was Toronto. But its quality of life does not just hinge on a low crime rate and good transport system. It's a culturally progressive, vibrant city, housing some of the world's best recent architectural developments. The bars and restaurants are right up there with the finest, especially in the area around King Street West, with venue after venue demonstrating a top-level synthesis of innovative design, food and drinks. West Lounge and Brant House are highly praised, but Blowfish is perhaps the single place that says the most about contemporary, cosmopolitan Toronto, which is why it is so often used for high-profile events, such as the premiere party for *Lost in Translation* and launches for Hugo Boss and Cartier. The name Blowfish suits Torontonians desire for the world to see their city as an adventurous destination. After all, the fish is a poisonous delicacy that has to be eaten with some bravura.

Johnson Chou's design is so thoughtfully integrated that the first word that comes to mind is sublime; but Blowfish also has the electric charge, the unquantifiable vibe that accompanies a restaurant or bar that is sure in the knowledge of both its expertise and popularity. It's no accident that many of the best-designed new restaurants in the world specialise in sushi. The artistry of this dish – the careful combination of colours, textures and flavours, along with the precision that often goes into its presentation – is born of some of the same aesthetics that can engender good design. Sushi and the style that has come to be somewhat lazily called Zen minimalist are first cousins. But really good design, whether of buildings, interiors, food or cocktails, is also often a discourse with a very particular, local environment, and this is where Blowfish excels.

The menu of chef GQ Pan may be Japanese at heart, but also draws on Toronto's own history with North American, European and pan-Asian influences – dishes such as Cajun-spiced tuna, Nigiri d'Alsace or Seafood Foie Gras Miso point the way. While the restaurant, like the bar, specialises in saké, it also recommends adventurous, fusion-led pairings, such as a Canadian Riesling with a honey-poached Asian pear. The medley of influences infuses Johnson Chou's design. Blowfish is housed in the traditional, neoclassical facade of a former Bank of Toronto

BLOWFISH RESTAURANT & SAKÉ BAR, TORONTO

BLOWFISH RESTAURANT & SAKÉ BAR
668 KING STREET WEST,
TORONTO, ONTARIO
M5V 1M7, CANADA

TEL +1 416 860 0606
WWW.BLOWFISHRESTAURANT.COM

THE DESIGNER:
JOHNSON CHOU

BLOWFISH IS THE FIRST RESTAURANT PROJECT FOR JOHNSON CHOU INC, A MULTIDISCIPLINARY ARCHITECTURE & DESIGN PRACTICE WHICH IS TAKING A LEADING ROLE IN TORONTO'S DESIGN BOOM. OF BLOWFISH, JOHNSON CHOU SAYS, 'INSPIRED BY THE NOTION OF FUSION CUISINE – A SYNTHESIS OF DISTINCT & OFTEN DIVERGENT CUISINES – THE IMAGE OF THE SPACE IS ARCHITECTURALLY INTERPRETED AS A DIALECTIC OF OPPOSITES, EVOCATIVE OF THE FUSION OR SYNTHESIS OF EASTERN & WESTERN ARCHITECTURE & THEIR RESPECTIVE FORMS, MATERIALS, TEXTURES & ICONOGRAPHY.'

building, and inside Chou has created a juxtaposition of East and West. Traditional, crystal chandeliers bring out the tall grandeur of the room but overhang sparer furniture designs, with wooden tables augmented only by a central groove and in-built chopstick rests.

Japanese shoji screens are evoked with a virtually translucent metal-mesh curtain differentiating the main restaurant area from the backlit bar, which has a luxurious onyx counter running the length of the space. Sandwiched between the screen and the counter, the bar space is simply a runway strip – very Japanese. The lounge adjoins the restaurant area, with low pouffes and banquettes surrounding miniature versions of the boxy dining tables.

The design may be largely minimalist in ethos but walnut panelling, coloured floor-lighting and an intimate scale give the restaurant warmth. Continuing the hybridised or 'fusion' theme (which even extends to the excellently designed unisex toilets), the space is adaptable, with the dining area becoming a very popular lounge bar, with in-house DJ, once the kitchen is closed. The speciality saké cocktails come into their own then, with favourites including the Typhoon Season: saké, vodka, mango juice and lychee liqueur.

MURANO
URBAN RESORT

The Murano Urban Resort, a Parisian hotel with a thriving, hip restaurant and bar, takes its name and inspiration from the glass-makers of the island of Murano, near Venice, whose work has long been associated with luxury and high design. One of the Murano's many surprises is that it has an all-white theme (which is carried through most impressively in the restaurant) while Murano glass is often associated with the use of colour. The interior designers are Christine Derory and Raymond Morel, whose successes include the Villa Royale Place Pigalle. The achievement of the design, which is reminiscent of the Philippe Starck–Ian Schrager combo, is to combine a very contemporary shock factor with traditional expectations of luxury, quality and comfort. The restaurant, which opened in 2004, is one of the most impressive parts of the hotel, and along with the bar lounge has garnered a reputation as a destination for stylish Parisians. It is situated in the continually trendy Marais area where, although the mood may be coolly relaxed, expectations are high and the competition is increasingly fierce.

Both the bar and the restaurant are made to feel exclusive as they are hidden by white-draped doorways off the hotel's lounge, which itself makes a cool-meets-grand setting for a cocktail or glass of champagne. Set beneath a skylight, the lounge has a tremendous, stretched, white-leather Chesterfield sofa running in front of a similarly elongated 6-metre fireplace which brings a blaze of colour to the mostly white setting. Other seating is provided by grey-leather Jasmine chairs by Corinto. Together, the bar, lounge and restaurant spaces are the social heart of the building, and this area is its axis.

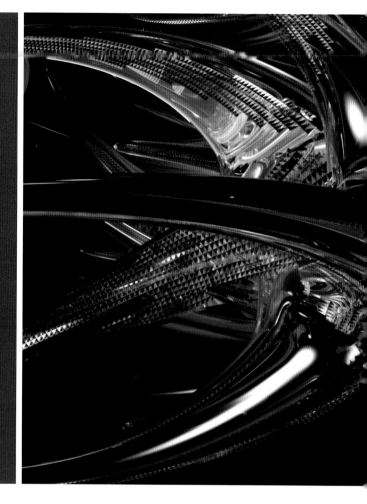

IN THE MIX:
MURANO GLASS

GLASS-MAKING WAS SUCH A HUGE INDUSTRY IN VENICE THAT IN 1291, THE ARTISANS WERE MOVED OUT TO THE ISLAND OF MURANO AS A PRECAUTION AGAINST FIRE. EVER SINCE, MURANO HAS BEEN THE WORLDWIDE CAPITAL OF LUXURIOUS GLASS MANUFACTURE & ITS MASTER GLASS-BLOWERS RANK ALONGSIDE THE CREATIVE GENIUSES OF ANY ART FORM. MURANO-GLASS CHANDELIERS ARE AN IMMEDIATE SIGNIFIER OF TRADITIONAL OPULENCE, & CONSEQUENTLY THEY ARE INCORPORATED INTO THE INTERIORS OF MANY LUXURY HOTELS, BARS & RESTAURANTS THROUGHOUT THE WORLD. HOWEVER, INSPIRED BY THE SUCCESS OF ARTISTS SUCH AS DALE CHIHULY WHO MERGED THE LONG-STANDING CRAFTSMANSHIP WITH CONTEMPORARY DESIGN, DESIGNERS ARE NOW INCORPORATING MURANO GLASS IN EVEN THE MOST RADICAL INTERIORS, AS THE MURANO URBAN RESORT SHOWS.

The restaurant comprises a striking, 5-metre-high main dining room along with two smaller rooms and a sun terrace. The impact of the main room is immediate, with a ceiling hung with white, glass cylinders suspended at different heights. Along with tall, white, window drapes and the light, Carrara marble floor, the cylinders make the restaurant seem like a secret ice cave. Blood-red armchairs provide the only constant source of colour, but light in a variation of different hues pulses through the regiment of icicles. At the back, a further room has been raised so it provides a vantage point over the main restaurant area. Here, the walls are decorated with circles of light, while specially designed Murano-glass pendant lamps wriggle down from the ceiling. The innovative, mainly Mediterranean-style menu, surprisingly good for vegetarians, has been created by Julien Chicoisne, formerly of Fermes de Marie in Megève, along with Pierre Auge, who worked under the legendary Pierre Gagnaire at Sketch in London.

MURANO URBAN RESORT, PARIS

MURANO URBAN RESORT
13 BOULEVARD DU TEMPLE,
PARIS 75003, FRANCE

TEL +33 (0)1 42 712000
WWW.MURANORESORT.COM

CLASSIC COCKTAILS:
FRENCH MARTINI

ONE OF THE GREAT CLASSIC TWISTS ON A TRADITIONAL MARTINI
COCKTAIL IS THE FRENCH MARTINI, WHICH IS A RASPBERRY-
FLAVOURED LIQUEUR.

INGREDIENTS:
50 ML (1.5 OZ) BOMBAY SAPPHIRE GIN
50 ML (1.5 OZ) PINEAPPLE JUICE
10 ML (0.3 OZ) RASPBERRY LIQUER

METHOD:
SHAKE & STRAIN
GLASS: MARTINI
GARNISH: NONE

The links to the bright colours of Murano glass are very much in evidence in the bar, which has coloured padded wall-panels featuring a single, central stud, and a ceiling of suspended, coloured discs. A constantly changing display of images is projected above the 15-metre-long, slate bar counter. The counter itself provides an interesting twist on bar conventions. From the customer's point of view, it is at regular table height, fronted by low pod chairs rather than bar stools. On the other side, the bar staff are at a lower level so they are standing while serving the seated guests. Perversely, tall stools are reserved for the high inox tables of the main area: the result makes an interesting play on dimensions. Late at night, a pianist gives way to DJs, and the video display comes into its own in helping to create a funky, music-lounge setting. The bar offers aperitifs, cocktails and over a hundred types of vodka, along with a good choice of cigars.

BLUE BAR

Dublin-born designer David Collins rarely puts a foot wrong, despite his willingness to go out on a limb and stir up a little controversy. The Blue Bar, an exceedingly popular haunt of the rich, famous and downright stylish ever since it opened at the Berkeley Hotel in 1999, is such a beautifully serene and luxurious space that at first it is hard to comprehend just how daring it is. It is said that Madonna has had the design replicated in her own home, while fashion designer John Galliano calls it his 'favourite home from home'. That may be a bit of a stretch for those of us who don't have achingly cool drawing rooms in our own abodes, but at least we can all share the benefit of relaxing with a cocktail or slowly perusing the list of 50 whiskies in this intimate, unhurried space.

A beguiling mix of the contemporary and the traditional informs the whole design and has made the bar a perfect place for the reawakening of cocktail culture. The customers are stylish and adventurous, choosing from an excellent cocktail list that includes both classics and new departures. The bar menu features modern twists on tapas, such as queenie scallops with wasabi and lime vinaigrette which, like the bar itself, are small and perfectly formed. The bar has also positioned itself for the re-emergence of cigar culture, which has risen in popularity alongside the clamorous demands for total smoking bans. The Blue Bar has a 'Grape and Smoke' menu which matches particular wines with cigars – a contemporary twist on a traditional English sensibility that is typical of the Blue Bar. However, the cigar-puffing customers are more likely to be young women in Manolo Blahniks than old gents in smoking jackets.

THE DESIGNER: DAVID COLLINS

'MY BRIEF WAS TO ESTABLISH A DESIGN CONCEPT THAT WAS IN KEEPING WITH THE BERKELEY BUT WITH SOME CONTEMPORARY VIBE,' SAYS DAVID COLLINS, DESIGNER OF THE BLUE BAR. ONE OF LONDON'S FOREMOST BAR & RESTAURANT DESIGNERS, HE HAS ALSO PERFORMED HIS MAGIC AT CLARIDGE'S BAR, AGAIN BLENDING CONTEMPORARY DESIGN WITH HISTORICAL REFERENCES. BORN NEAR DUBLIN, WITH EACH PROJECT HE AIMS TO FIND 'A SOPHISTICATED COUNTERPOINT BETWEEN RATIONALE & AESTHETIC' – IN OTHER WORDS, THE DESIGN HAS GOT TO BE BEAUTIFUL BUT ALSO 'WORK' FOR HIS CLIENTS & THEIR CUSTOMERS. OTHER PROJECTS INCLUDE THE CELEBRITY NIGHTCLUB KABARET'S PROPHECY, WHICH FEATURES ANIMATED DESIGNS BY JAMIE HEWLETT, LOCANDA LOCATELLI, THE WOLSELEY & J SHEEKEY.

The Blue Bar's name may give the game away but the décor is still a surprise. It is a monochrome delight, where the emphasis on a single colour has been restrained from becoming visually overbearing by dextrous subtlety. The blue walls verge on typical Wedgwood, but have been given a gentle warmth by brushing red powder into the delicately cracked paint. Comparisons to Wedgwood could continue, but whereas the china often features white swags, the intricate carvings on the Blue Bar's walls are the same colour as the background. David Collins has called the colour Lutyens Blue. Its name highlights the designer's strength of character. The wood panelling and carvings, designed by Sir Edwin Lutyens (1869–1944), survive from the original Berkeley before the hotel relocated to its current, purpose-built home in 1972. In the new hotel building, designed by Martin O'Rourke, they were placed in a sitting room which became known as the Lutyens Room. In turning the room into the Blue Bar, Collins took the hotel's main historical feature and covered it with blue paint. Some followers of Lutyens, a prestigious architect whose work includes Drogo Castle, the Viceroy's House in New Delhi and the Cenotaph, think of Collins' decision to paint the intricate carvings as sacrilege. For others, Collins has brought the carvings alive again, giving both the room – and the reputation of the Berkeley – a contemporary zing.

Far from being deliberately outrageous, Collins has tipped his hat with respect to Lutyens throughout the design. The cardinal's hat light in the centre of the ceiling's white, decorated recess is based on one of Lutyens' own

BLUE BAR, LONDON

THE BLUE BAR
THE BERKELEY,
WILTON PLACE,
KNIGHTSBRIDGE,
LONDON SW1X 7RL, UK

TEL +44 (0)20 7235 6000
WWW.THE-BERKELEY.CO.UK

designs, while the black, crocodile leather flooring and black chair frames allude to the architect's repeated use of the colour. The bar's drawing-room design also refers to Lutyens' reputation as one of the foremost designers of English country houses. The counter is often the focus of bar design, but here it is placed at the end of the room and blends into the overall scheme, aided by the lightness of the onyx counter-top and the setting of the bottle displays into two bookshelf-like recesses. It isn't allowed to dominate the room, encouraging the guests to think of the bar as a private sitting room.

As well as drawing on faux-Renaissance influences, the Blue Bar is also inspired by Art Deco, the design style which will always be associated with the golden age of the cocktail. The blue-leather, sloping-back chairs, and large Modern rug add an air of comfort, glamour and worldly sophistication that make it hard to move on to another bar. The secret to the Blue Bar's success is that although it is protected by a doorman and prices are just about as steep as you find in London, inside it is a calm, unpretentious oasis where everyone from celebrities to local fashionistas to the hotel guests are treated as equal. The witty design ensures its continued popularity because its blend of history, tradition, contemporariness and risk allows it to be unique and timeless, with no hint of wannabe desperation.

CAMPBELL
APARTMENT

In a city perhaps more dedicated to cocktail culture than any other, the Campbell Apartment in New York's Grand Central station is probably the single best place to enjoy a classic cocktail. The setting is perfect.

With its grand size, landmark status and bustling comings and goings, Grand Central itself is a monument to the romantic ideals of America. Opening in 1913, the Beaux-Arts building, bedecked by a 50-foot-long pediment and statues of Minerva, Hercules and Mercury, features a 375-foot-long main concourse beneath a ceiling decorated as a star-filled night sky. The Campbell Apartment, set amongst the blocks that surround the terminal, shares in its stately grandeur. It is named after John W Campbell, a famous tycoon and chairman of the Credit Clearing House who had his private office and salon in the apartment from 1923 to the 1940s. At the time, it was thought to be one of the most impressive offices in New York, and Campbell used it to impress guests at evening soirees. Following its sympathetic conversion in 1999, it is now one of the city's most impressive, upscale bars.

Set in a single room, the bar's 20-foot-high, decorated marble walls rise up from wooden panelling at their base towards a beautiful Florentine ceiling of intricately painted wooden beams. The wooden bar counter is placed before a huge, leaded-glass window, but the bottle display is simply housed on the long windowshelf so that it does not detract from the window's glory. Original features include an immense stone fireplace, standing behind Mr Campbell's own sturdy, black safe. At one end, a carved balcony rests on top of wooden panelling and provides a view of the sophisticated merriment below.

CLASSIC COCKTAILS: MANHATTAN

SAID TO HAVE BEEN CREATED FOR LADY JENNY CHURCHILL, WINSTON CHURCHILL'S MOTHER, AT THE MANHATTAN CLUB IN AROUND 1890, THE MANHATTAN HAS BECOME ESTABLISHED AS ONE OF THE ALL-TIME CLASSICS. VARIATIONS INCLUDE A PERFECT MANHATTAN, WITH A MIX OF SWEET & DRY VERMOUTH, A ROB ROY, WITH SCOTCH RATHER THAN BOURBON, & THE BRONX, MADE WITH GIN.

INGREDIENTS:
50 ML (1.5 OZ) BOURBON OR RYE WHISKY
30 ML (1 OZ) SWEET VERMOUTH
DASH OF BITTERS

METHOD:
STIR WITH ICE & STRAIN
GLASS: MARTINI
GARNISH:
MARASCHINO CHERRY

For the furnishings, the Medici style gives way to a mixture of Moroccan and English-club influences. Dark wooden tables are accompanied by club-style chairs and sofas, some of which are covered with slightly exotic, tapestry-like patterns which complement the blue, red and gold rug. The blue of the carpet is picked out by the leather scroll-seats of the stools that grace the bar counter. All in all, the space manages to effectively combine a sense of refined antiquity with modern comfort. It is a bar in which to enjoy the finer things in life – vintage wines, champagne and, of course, classic cocktails. It caters for current tastes and trends but, as befits the décor and ambience, it's strong on traditional cocktails. Naturally, it's a great place for a Manhattan but other favourites include its particularly potent Prohibition Punch involving rum, Grand Marnier, passion fruit juice and champagne.

COCKTAIL CONNECTIONS: ALL ABOUT EVE

*I ADMIT I MAY HAVE SEEN BETTER DAYS ... BUT I'M STILL NOT TO
BE HAD FOR THE PRICE OF A COCKTAIL LIKE A SALTED PEANUT*

ONE OF THE GREAT FILMS ABOUT THE BACK-STABBING WORLD OF NEW YORK'S BROADWAY IS *ALL ABOUT EVE* (1950) STARRING BETTE DAVIS AS MARGO CHANNING, A GREAT ACTRESS WITH A DRY, SOMETIMES MALICIOUS & ALWAYS SPIKY WIT. COCKTAILS & SPIRITS ARE OFTEN TO THE FORE, & ARE THE SUBJECT OF SOME OF THE FILM'S MANY KILLER QUOTES SUCH AS, 'THERE'S A MESSAGE FROM THE BARTENDER. DOES MISS CHANNING KNOW SHE ORDERED DOMESTIC GIN BY MISTAKE?' TO WHICH SHE REPLIES, 'THE ONLY THING I ORDERED BY MISTAKE IS THE GUESTS. THEY'RE DOMESTIC, TOO, & THEY DON'T CARE WHAT THEY DRINK AS LONG AS IT BURNS!'

CAMPBELL APARTMENT, NEW YORK

CAMPBELL APARTMENT
GRAND CENTRAL TERMINAL,
15 VANDERBILT AVENUE,
NEW YORK, NY 10017, USA

TEL +1 212 953 0409
WWW.HOSPITALITYHOLDINGS.COM

THE MIXOLOGIST:
DALE DeGROFF

AS WELL AS THE CAMPBELL APARTMENT, OTHER UPSCALE, TRADITIONAL NEW YORK HOTSPOTS FOR COCKTAILS INCLUDE BEMELMAN'S BAR AT THE CARLYLE HOTEL, THE KING COLE BAR AT THE ST REGIS & THE RAINBOW ROOM. DALE DEGROFF, SOMETIMES CALLED THE 'KING OF COCKTAILS', HONED HIS CRAFT AT THE RAINBOW ROOM FOLLOWING ITS RESTORATION IN 1987, CREATING OVER 400 DRINKS. HE HAS BECOME PERHAPS THE BEST-KNOWN COCKTAIL AFICIONADO IN THE WORLD. HE SAYS, 'THE SCENE IN THE COCKTAIL BUSINESS HAS NEVER BEEN MORE INTERESTING EXCEPT PERHAPS IN THE GOLDEN AGE OF THE COCKTAIL 1880 TO 1912. I STILL LOOK BACK TO THOSE YEARS FOR CREATIVE IDEAS & IT WILL BE MANY YEARS BEFORE THAT WELL RUNS DRY! ... I FIND TREMENDOUS INSPIRATION IN THE YOUNG PROFESSIONALS WHO HAVE EMBRACED THIS PROFESSION, NOT IN A NARROW WAY, BUT AS CONSUMMATE MASTERS STUDYING ALL ASPECTS OF BEVERAGE FROM COCKTAILS TO SPIRITS TO BEER, WINE & EXOTICS LIKE SAKÉ & SHOCHU.'

Outside on Vanderbilt Avenue Portico is the Campbell Apartment Terrace, which, like the bar, is owned by Hospitality Holdings whose other New York ventures include the World Bar in the Trump World Tower, the Carnegie Club and the Patio. Like the main bar, the Terrace specialises in classic cocktails such as a Gin-Berry Fizz. Set outdoors, the seating includes mahogany rocking chairs, a tribute to the original furniture in the women's lounges of Grand Central station.

Shortly after the Campbell Apartment opened the owner, Mark C Grossich of Hospitality Holdings, said, 'Usually, trendy means loud and abusive and intense. We do not want to be the flavour of the month or the year. We want to be in it for the long run.' Six years down the line, his wish seems to be coming true. While some ultra-contemporary bars suffer from having been momentarily all the rage, this bar's glorification of classic sensibilities serves it well.

CAFÉ & DINING JP

Café & Dining JP was originally known as J-Pop Café Odaiba when it opened in 2002. The name may have changed, but the design and the purpose is just the same, keying in to the J-Pop (Japanese pop music) phenomenon which has remained largely insular to Japan. Unusually, the unadulterated love of pop music carries no embarrassment in Japan until well past the mid-30s. The small J-Pop Café chain and now Café & Dining JP have a design sophistication which appeals to a very cognisant, older market. A similar European or American venture would involve cheap, glitter ball sparkles and loud, eye-catching motifs aimed at a 13-year-old with an attention deficit disorder. By contrast, Café & Dining JP may be dotted with music video screens both large and small but it looks a high-style bar and club for well-heeled fashionistas. The design concept created by Katsunori Suzuki is innovative, intelligent and elegantly resolved while drinks include saké cocktails. This is no Hard Rock Café either.

Suzuki, who also designed the original J-Pop Café in the Shibuya district of Tokyo, has created a futuristic, biomorphic design for the venture which is situated on the fifth floor of Sega's Joy Polis arcade. This forms part of the Decks Tokyo Beach entertainment and shopping complex which is built on reclaimed land in Odaiba and is simultaneously helping to alleviate Tokyo's restrictive space problems while forming a new leisure destination. The exterior of Café & Dining JP establishes the motif of organic futurism with a green-neon-lit wall of almost 2,000, regimented egg-like spheres looking like a spread of sci-fi caviar. Inside, the shell of the spaces is rounded and amorphous, with tendrils, trunk-like pillars and tables emerging from the walls. The main material is white,

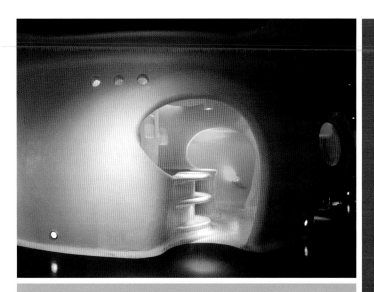

CAFÉ & DINING JP, TOKYO

FIFTH FLOOR, DECKS BEACH TOKYO,
ODAIBA 1-6-1, MINATO-KU,
TOKYO 135-0091, JAPAN

TEL +81 (0)3 3570 5767

IN THE MIX: SHOCHU

J-POP, JAPAN'S OWN BRAND OF POP MUSIC WHICH INSPIRED CAFÉ & DINING JP, MAY NOT HAVE TAKEN THE WORLD BY STORM BUT THERE IS A GROWING APPRECIATION OF OTHER FACETS OF JAPANESE CULTURE, PARTICULARLY FOOD AND DRINK. FIRST SAKÉ AND NOW SHOCHU HAVE SUDDENLY BECOME POPULAR WORLDWIDE IN RECENT TIMES. LIKE SAKÉ, SHOCHU IS DISTILLED FROM RICE BUT CAN BE BASED ON WHEAT, CANE OR SWEET POTATO. A VODKA-LIKE, INFUSED SPIRIT, IT WAS FORMERLY A WORKING MAN'S DRINK, WHICH PROBABLY ORIGINATED IN AROUND THE 14TH CENTURY. IT IS FINDING A WIDER AUDIENCE IN JAPAN AND IS NOW BECOMING THE DRINK OF COOL YOUNG HIPSTERS IN CALIFORNIA AND LONDON, WHO ARE DOWNING CHU-HAI SHOCHU COCKTAILS. A BAR SIMPLY CALLED SHOCHU LOUNGE AND SPECIALISING IN COCKTAILS MADE FROM THE SPIRIT WAS NAMED LONDON'S 2005 BAR OF THE YEAR BY *TIME OUT*. THE BAR'S SIGNATURE DRINKS INCLUDE THE TOKYO BABY, COMPRISING SHOCHU, WHITE PEACH AND CALPICO MIX.

fibreglass-reinforced gypsum which allows for both sturdy fixtures and the necessary flexibility to create the curvaceous forms. Most of the colour comes from the lighting and from the video screens. Controls are integrated into some of the seating so customers can select their own choice of music videos, but, with an emphasis on creative dishes and relaxation it's easy to forget the original purpose of JP. Indeed, Suzuki himself has stated that he 'avoided designing a space directly related to the music scene. The café is first and foremost a place to eat good food in a relaxing atmosphere.'

As the name suggests, Café & Dining JP is split into two main areas, with one area – the Bio Forest Zone – leaning towards fast food and the other acting more as a restaurant/bar. Past the Bio Forest counter, there is an open-air terrace, but the real glory of Café & Dining JP is the main dining and bar area, the Bio Cave, which also provides excellent views of Tokyo Bay. Accessed through a curving cave-tunnel, the restaurant's main focus is its exterior walls, made of large sheets of glass above a long, curving counter. The counter acts as a table which curves out into the room and also provides the base of the angled, tree-trunk

pillars that support the roof. The organic, amorphous shape of the counter is set off by a line of classic white Panton chairs with their one-piece design that swoops up from the floor and curves back on itself to form the seat and back rest. As night falls, these seats, with their unimpaired views of the bay area, are the prime spot for a cocktail, but sitting elsewhere is no less of a designer statement as the chairs are Philippe Starck's rounded, Soft Egg design and Karim Rashid's Oh-Chair. The space is largely open, but more private areas are provided by a curvaceous row of red leather and white booths beneath a line of video screens. Throughout, mood is created by a LED light display of alternating colours.

Customers entering from the Joy Polis arcade pass the green egg-wall and find the Bio Forest Zone curving away to the right. This is the fast food area, featuring white tables and black Oh-Chairs, a screen made up of nine monitors above a stage, a DJ booth and further individual monitors set into large portholes sticking out from the wall. On the curving walls opposite, further portholes are glazed, allowing coloured light to seep into the space.

MOO

Restaurant Moo, the less formal MooVida and their joint cocktail bar Moodern together form an excellent enterprise in the Hotel Omm, Barcelona. The hotel is owned by Grupo Tragaluz, the most high-profile restaurateurs in Barcelona, whose approach has been rather like the Zetter Restaurant & Rooms in London: the guestrooms are beautifully designed but the heart of the enterprise is indubitably a fantastic restaurant and bar aimed at fashionable locals. Restaurant Moo has gone down a storm since it opened in late 2003, not least because it is managed by the Roca brothers, famous for running El Celler de Can Roca in Girona which ranks right up alongside El Bulli as the finest gastronomic experience in Spain.

Part of the reason Grupo Traguluz has established such a good reputation amongst the Barceloneses has been its desire to match good design and ambience with intelligent menus. By comparison to many other countries, Spain doesn't yet have quite the same fascination with high-concept designs of bars and restaurants, but the group is leading the way. Moo may not be showy but it is extremely cleverly designed and incorporates some arresting visual features. Set at the rear of the hotel, the restaurant space could be dark and unpromising but, aided by an interior courtyard, it is welcoming, light and airy. The courtyard itself is very small and could have ended up as an unusable, dead space but it has been turned into a light tunnel with the help of white paint and stainless-steel reflector shields. With different sizes mounted at various angles on the wall, these shields are combined with tall bamboo canes to create an interesting sculptural artwork that acts as a backdrop to the restaurant. Inside, further light has

been brought into the space through a series of electronically adjustable, angular skylights which pierce through the ceiling. They make a very distinctive architectural feature. The mixture of round and rectangular black tables is surrounded by Jorge Pensi's elegant Kayak chairs in both black and bleached-wood versions. A floating, virtually translucent metal-mesh screen helps to create a partial division between the restaurant and the rest of the ground floor. Overall, the effect is to offer a simple but stylish setting for the experimental Catalan menu designed by the Roca brothers. The cuisine sets up an exploration of tastes through either degustation menus or a series of à la carte half-portions that allow the diners to try a broad range of flavours, which include the Roca classic warm foie gras with honey, brioche, vanilla and saffron milk mousse. Careful consideration is given to pairing wines with particular courses.

Away from the restaurant, virtually the whole of the ground floor on Hotel Omm is a social space. Grupo Traguluz wanted Omm to be part of the Barcelona scene, rather than an insular tourist enclave and you could easily miss the small reception on the right-hand side and believe you were in just an upmarket lounge bar and restaurant.

MOO, BARCELONA

MOO RESTAURANT
HOTEL OMM, ROSELLÓ 265,
08008 BARCELONA, SPAIN

TEL +34 934 454 000
WWW.HOTELOMM.ES OR WWW.DESIGNHOTELS.COM

COCKTAIL CONNECTIONS: LUIS BUÑUEL

IF YOU WERE TO ASK ME IF I'D EVER HAD THE BAD LUCK TO MISS MY DAILY COCKTAIL, I'D HAVE TO SAY THAT I DOUBT IT; WHERE CERTAIN THINGS ARE CONCERNED, I PLAN AHEAD.

LUIS BUÑUEL (1900-83), THE FATHER OF SURREALIST FILMS & TO SOME THE GREATEST SPANISH FILM-MAKER OF ALL TIME, WAS BORN IN CALANDA IN THE NORTHEAST OF SPAIN IN 1900. THE CREATOR OF ENDURING CLASSICS SUCH AS *UN CHIEN ANDALOU* (1929) WHICH HE CO-WROTE WITH SALVADOR DALÍ, *BELLE DU JOUR* (1967) & *THE DISCREET CHARM OF THE BOURGEOISIE* (1972), BUÑUEL WAS A MARTINI AFICIONADO. HE WROTE IN HIS AUTOBIOGRAPHY *MY LAST SIGH* (1983), 'TO PROVOKE, OR SUSTAIN, A REVERIE IN A BAR, YOU HAVE TO DRINK ENGLISH GIN, ESPECIALLY IN THE FORM OF THE DRY MARTINI.'

Architect Juli Capella has created a compelling facade made of cabra marble, with peels of the limestone curving away from the exterior to allow light into the guestrooms. The ground floor, though, is fully glazed, inviting passers-by to enjoy the lounge and bar. The interior is by Sandra Tarruella and Isabel López Vilalta who have created a relaxed, grey lounge, making use of the double-height section of the lobby with immense, pink Oven lamps designed by Antoni Arola. Despite the height and the glazing, the lounge has a warm feel, aided by cushioned, Perobell sofas in grey and green and a horizontal fireplace set in a cut-through section of one of the interior walls. It's a very relaxed setting for cocktails. The bar itself, towards the rear, has two counters set together to form a black leather and metal rectangle. There are small cubic tables amongst the sofas but more formal table settings (again including Kayak chairs) are placed towards the back of the lounge for those who want to choose from MooVida's menu of healthy, seasonal dishes. The heart of MooVida is another black, metal rectangle, which acts as a communal table for informal dining. Like the rest of Omm, it manages to combine good produce and good design with an informality that appeals to well-heeled but carefree Barceloneses.

The rituals of the geisha in Japanese society may be part of a mysterious, half-hidden world, but the Hollywood restaurant Geisha House brings sexuality to the fore, and in the process has become one of Tinseltown's most treasured A-list restaurants. It helps when your investors include hot, young and handsome properties from the film and TV industry such as Ashton Kutcher, Dulé Hill of *The West Wing* and Christopher Masterson of *Malcom in the Middle*, whose involvement does nothing to detract from the virility of the enterprise. Robert de Niro brought great kudos to investing in restaurants with his involvement in Nobu; many actors and restaurateurs are now finding mutual benefits in partnering up for restaurants that offer high style, glamour and good food. It's all a long way from Planet Hollywood.

Geisha House is a modern Japanese restaurant, sushi bar and saké lounge that sets out to draw on Japanese tradition while creating a unique setting that would appeal to glamorous Hollywood sophists. It's red, dark and sexy in a manner very untypical of our established idea of Japanese restaurants. Thematically, it explores the traditions of the geisha, the professional female companions trained in the arts of music, dancing and conversation. There is often a coyness attached to discussing what the geishas are also trained in, but Geisha House addresses it full on – figuratively speaking, at this titillating establishment the kimonos lack their sashes. The training of a geisha takes many years, developing through various stages which are here represented by different saké cocktails, with the 'Shikomo', named after the very first stage of

INSPIRED CREATIONS: THE BLUSHING GEISHA

MIXOLOGIST JAMIE WALKER CREATED THE BLUSHING GEISHA COCKTAIL SPECIFICALLY FOR GEISHA HOUSE, WHICH ALSO HAS AN IMPRESSIVE LIST OF SAKÉ COCKTAILS.

INGREDIENTS:
50 ML (1.5 OZ) BOMBAY SAPPHIRE GIN
25 ML (0.75 OZ) LYCHEE JUICE
25 ML (0.75 OZ) POMEGRANATE JUICE
15 ML (0.5 OZ) SAKÉ
10 ML (0.3 OZ) GRENADINE
5 ML (0.15 OZ) LIME

METHOD:
SHAKE WITH ICE & STRAIN
INTO A CHILLED GLASS
GLASS: MARTINI
GARNISH: TWIST OF LIME

apprenticeship, featuring saké, Midori, lemon and Japanese cucumber, and the 'Maiko', the main, final training stage, blending Asian pear saké, orange and fresh ginger. The geisha device is original and does add a sexy allure to the Geisha House experience, but the restaurant can only maintain the giddy heights of its popularity if this is merely the dressing on highly creditable food and design. Fortunately, there are no worries on either front.

Geisha House is designed by Tag Front, who also designed the Balboa Restaurant on Sunset Boulevard, and Scott Oster. Split into different areas and levels, it is linked by several monumental pieces including a red tower inset with raised fireplaces, a huge mural of a cityscape adorned with Japanese banners, a long saké bar-counter and a wall of screens showing different visual elements of Japanese culture. Old and new Japan are brought together, with elements of Western-style luxury also thrown into the mix. Mandi Raferty of Tag Front says that they set out to 'capture a Japanese and Geisha feel but to stay clear of what is normally associated with an American interpretation of Japanese style'. This is reminiscent of the ambitions of Megu, the acclaimed New York restaurant that appears on the CV of both the chef and the manager of Geisha House. Both designs are theatrical, and use

THE MIXOLOGIST: JAMIE WALKER

JAMIE WALKER, CREATOR OF THE BLUSHING GEISHA COCKTAIL FOR GEISHA HOUSE, HAS RUN SOME OF LONDON'S BEST COCKTAIL BARS INCLUDING CIRCUS & ALPHABET, AND HAS ALSO TRAINED STAFF AT MANY OF THE LEGENDARY BARS OF RECENT TIMES SUCH AS THE ATLANTIC BAR & GRILL, THE LONG BAR AT THE SANDERSON & LAB. DESPITE BEING INVOLVED IN TRAINING, HE BELIEVES THAT INDIVIDUALITY IS THE KEY TO CREATIVE MIXOLOGY: 'THE INGREDIENTS HAVE TO BE RESPECTED. BEYOND THAT, YOU DO IT YOUR WAY. EXPERIMENT, BE ADVENTUROUS, GET THINGS WRONG, CHALLENGE THE RULES, & MAKE THE RECIPES YOUR OWN.' THE GLOBAL AMBASSADOR FOR BOMBAY SAPPHIRE, HE'S A FAN OF THE CLASSIC MARTINI BUT CURRENT FAVOURITES ALSO INCLUDE A PEAR & ELDERFLOWER COLLINS.

traditional Japanese textures and images in an unusual, contemporary way, but the similarities end there. Even though they share a vision that fuses innovative food, stylishness and impressive interiors that defy nationalist stereotypes, the end results are divergent and unique.

The menu devised by the chef, Genichi Mizoguchi, includes Japanese tapas-style dishes as well as contemporary takes on sushi and sashimi. Having the choices arranged on a 'tapas-style' menu, where the diner can choose a variety of smaller dishes, is essentially a way of reintroducing the usual Eastern tradition in a format that Westerners can readily understand. Japanese cuisine suits being eaten this way, with the emphasis placed on a wide range of subtle flavours and different textures rather than on a huge portion of one dish. As co-owner Lonnie Moore says, 'The traditional Japanese dining experience has no set rhythm', indicating that Geisha House is a free-flowing experience uninhibited by a three-course format. The rhythm that does exist in Geisha House is created by continual allusions to sensuality.

COCKTAIL CONNECTIONS: SWINGERS

THE 1996 INDEPENDENT COMEDY *SWINGERS* SOON BECAME A COCKTAIL CULT ON BOTH SIDES OF THE ATLANTIC. SET IN LOS ANGELES, IT FOLLOWS AN ACTOR WHO HAS FAILED TO MAKE IT AS A STAR & ALSO LOST HIS GIRLFRIEND. HIS FRIENDS TRY & PICK HIM UP ON A TOUR OF THE LA LOUNGE-BAR SCENE, SUPPING MANY A FINE COCKTAIL ON THE WAY. EVEN THE MOVIE POSTER FEATURES A HUGE MARTINI, WHILE THE TAGLINE IS 'COCKTAILS FIRST, QUESTIONS LATER.' ALWAYS A GOOD IDEA.

GEISHA HOUSE, HOLLYWOOD

GEISHA HOUSE
6633 HOLLYWOOD BOULEVARD
HOLLYWOOD
CA 90028
USA

TEL +1 323 460 6300
WWW.GEISHAHOUSEHOLLYWOOD.COM

BOND BAR

The Australian bar scene goes from strength to strength with the cities of Melbourne and Sydney rivalling each other to be the premier bar destination of the country. One of Melbourne's best bars, and by far the most architecturally significant, is Bond. Opening in 2001, it was one of the city's original leaders in bar style but has managed to remain popular amongst a rash of recent openings. Obviously, the name conjures up cocktail associations with James Bond, but the bar is very far from being a tacky, poster-strewn homage to 007, and is actually named after the street it's in. The bar does share with the film series a certain suavity, knowing sophistication and slick design but the obvious connections stop there. In fact, Bond is a wonderful exponent of an apparently ardently contemporary bar that has its design principles steeped in the golden age of the cocktail. With its warm chocolate and cream colours and luxurious textures, its high design is tempered by a leaning towards comfort and intimacy.

The bar is converted from an underground office space, but its original use is no longer detectable. The designer, Fady Hachem of Playground Melbourne, says, 'As a visual creation, Bond draws influences from Art Deco ideology combined with postmodernism.' This inspiration may be a little hard to grasp after a couple of Bond's carefully crafted cocktails, but it

COCKTAIL CONNECTIONS: JAMES BOND

THE CONNECTION BETWEEN JAMES BOND (SEEN HERE IN 2002'S *DIE ANOTHER DAY*) & MARTINIS HAS BEEN THERE FROM THE VERY FIRST FILM. IN *DR. NO* (1962), A WAITER AT THE JAMES'S HOTEL SAYS, 'ONE MEDIUM-DRY VODKA MARTINI, MIXED LIKE YOU SAID, SIR, NOT STIRRED.' 'SHAKEN, NOT STIRRED' HAS LONG BEEN A CATCHPHRASE FOR BOND LOVERS, ALTHOUGH A REQUEST TO SHAKE, RATHER THAN STIR, A MARTINI IS ENOUGH TO BRING FORTH A SNEER OF DERISION FROM MANY BARTENDERS. IN FACT, BOND'S SCRIPTWRITERS HAVE MADE HIM QUAFF A GREAT RANGE OF ALCOHOL IN HIS 20 FILMS, USUALLY WHILE ALSO EXPRESSING A SURPRISINGLY DETAILED KNOWLEDGE. HE HAS DRUNK SAKÉ, CHAMPAGNE, MINT JULEPS, BRANDY & SHERRY IN VARIOUS FILMS WHILE 2002'S *DIE ANOTHER DAY* SAW HIM CATCH UP WITH CURRENT COCKTAIL TASTES & ORDER A MOJITO.

provides the essence of how the bar manages to pull off the trick of being both starkly innovative in design terms but warm and embracing from a punter's point of view. The bar is vast, housing up to 500 customers in various sections over three levels, but even the main area is given an intimacy. The space is concave, with the walls curving outwards and then sweeping over to form the ceiling. The bottle display of the main bar and some of the seating in the dining area are cut into the curves of the walls, further establishing the integrated nature of the design and the feeling of a cocoon. The ceiling shape was the designer's alternative to having a broad flat expanse which would deaden the impact of the space. Rather than detracting from the interior, the ceiling was made into the design's principal feature.

The graceful curves and the use of veneers, hardwood and mirrors establish a 1930s concept of sublime elegance, but this is also a minimalist space which relies on simplicity, repeated motifs and relatively pared-down furnishings. The lighting adds to the sultry atmosphere, with uplights set into the curve of the walls to emphasise the concave and hooped structure of the bar.

BOND BAR
24 BOND STREET,
MELBOURNE,
VIC 3000, AUSTRALIA

TEL +61 (0)3 9629 9844
WWW.BONDLOUNGE.COM.AU

IN THE MIX: COGNAC

COGNAC, THE SPECIALIST DRINK OF THE BOND BAR, IS BRANDY THAT IS EXCLUSIVELY PRODUCED IN THE COGNAC/JARNAC AREA NORTH OF BORDEAUX, FRANCE. PARTICULARLY WHEN PRODUCED FROM GRAPES OF THE SPECIFIC GRANDE CHAMPAGNE SUB-REGION, IT PROVIDES ONE OF THE MOST EXPENSIVE TIPPLES TO BE FOUND IN THE WORLD. THE SHERATON PARK TOWER HOTEL IN LONDON CLAIMS TO SELL THE MOST EXPENSIVE COCKTAIL, THE LOUIS XIII DIAMOND, FEATURING LOUIS XIII COGNAC, CHARLES HEIDSIECK CHAMPAGNE, A DASH OF BITTERS & ... A DIAMOND. A COCKTAIL WITH A ONE-CARAT DIAMOND COSTS AROUND $7,000.

Different surfaces, including tiling and pressed-metals sheets on the walls, help give a distinctive mood to the various areas. As well as the dining area, which has finned tube-lights overhanging the tables, Bond has various specialist areas, not least of which is the Powder Room, decorated like a theatre dressing room and offering the services of hairdressers and beauticians. In the private lounge area, which features a shimmering, molten wall behind the bar, members can partake of specialist cognacs, single malt whiskies and cigars while, slightly creepily, viewing what's going on in the main bar through CCTV. There is also a dance floor, with audio and video projector ports available throughout the space so that function and mood can easily be altered.

All in all, Bond provides a perfect setting for the variety of specialist tastes which are finding a rapidly growing and informed young audience. Cocktails, though, are the main draw for most people, with trained bartenders offering a huge variety of concoctions. In 2002 the bar won 2002 Bar of the Year awards from both the *Age* newspaper and the Australian Liquor Industry Association.

JAMIE WALKER'S RECOMMENDED TOOLS & TECHNIQUES

BAR TOOLS

COCKTAIL SHAKER

The two-piece Boston Shaker is recommended over the three-piece shaker (i.e. one that consists of an all-metal beaker, strainer and cap). The Boston Shaker is made up of a glass beaker and a metal beaker. The glass beaker can be used to prepare ingredients without conducting warmth in the way metal does, thus ensuring an optimally chilled cocktail.

STRAINER

The Boston shaker requires a separator to drain the ingredients into a glass. If necessary, ingredients can be double-strained by holding a tea strainer beneath the regular cocktail strainer. This will remove any smaller, unwanted piths, seeds, etc.

BAR SPOON

A bar spoon is essential for layering and stirring your cocktails. The best ones will have a twisted stem and flat end to enable complete control.

MUDDLER

A wooden muddler is an important bar tool. If one is not available the end of a small wooden rolling pin or wooden-spoon handle will suffice although this may scar the glass if used too vigorously.

TECHNIQUES

BLENDING
Use this technique to create smooth frozen drinks. On the whole, blended drinks will contain more robust ingredients, such as juices, coconut cream and cream. You should place all the cocktail ingredients in the blender and blitz until the mixture is of a smooth consistency. It should hold two straws upright but still be thin enough to drink.

BUILDING THE DRINK
This is the simplest method of cocktail creating. Just pour all the ingredients into an ice-filled glass then give them a quick stir to gently mix them together.

CITRUS FLAME
Take a slightly larger section of skin than required for the twist. The top of the fruit is the best area as it is slightly harder. Hold the skin over the surface of the drink, facing it away from yourself. Take a lighter and warm the outside of the skin for about three seconds, then, keeping the flame lit, squeeze the skin. This will release the oils which ignite over the drink. This not only looks spectacular but also caramelises the sugars in the fruit, enhancing the cocktail's flavour.

CHILLING A MARTINI GLASS
Take a polished Martini glass and place a scoop of ice inside. Add water to the brim. Leave to chill whilst mixing your cocktail. When your cocktail is ready to strain, discard the ice and shake the glass to remove any excess water. By chilling the glass you will extend the life expectancy of the cocktail.

ICE

Never overlook the importance of ice. It is not only there to chill your drink but is also an integral ingredient. Always use fresh ice (the colder the better) as it has a more transparent appearance than 'tired weeping ice' which has a hazier look about it. If possible, keep ice in a professional ice bucket/well as this ensures that it is in a space which allows it to drain. This enables the ice to remain fresh for as long as possible.

INGREDIENTS

You should aim to use only the freshest, seasonal and regional ingredients. Juices should never be concentrated, but always freshly pressed or squeezed. Use no more than six ingredients – less is more – and make sure that they all have a proper function.

MUDDLING

This method uses a muddler to crush and macerate whole fruits, skins, sugars or herbs to release their juices and flavours. This normally takes place in the cocktail glass itself but can also happen in the shaker. If you do not own a muddler, you can use a flat-ended rolling pin.

SHAKE AND STRAIN

This method works beautifully with libations that contain cream, milk, juices, purées or egg. You should use the maximum amount of ice (this is to prevent dilution) and shake vigorously until the metal section of the shaker is well frosted. Vigorous shaking is especially important for cocktails containing egg white, so that the frothy head desired is created. Always use fresh ice in the finished glass as opposed to the ice you have just shaken and strain the ingredients into the glass using a cocktail strainer.

STIR AND STRAIN

This method works best for cocktails that need to be treated with a slightly defter hand than 'shaken' ones. The stirring should be done with the maximum amount of ice in the glass section of your shaker. This stops the drink becoming diluted or 'bruised' (with shaking, shards of ice and pockets of air damage the alcohol). The stirred ingredients should be strained into the relevant glass using a cocktail strainer.

SUGAR

To make sugar syrup, pour white granulated sugar into a saucepan. Add a little water to begin with, then add more as required, reducing the mixture to a syrupy consistency over a medium heat. Sugar syrup can be stored in the fridge for a short period of time. For spiced sugar, take 500g of plain white sugar. Add 15g of ground nutmeg, 15g of cinnamon and the seeds of 3 vanilla pods and stir well.

TWISTS

Using a sharp knife remove a section of skin about 10 mm wide and 25 mm long from the required fruit sliver. Always remove as much of the pith as possible. Then take a sliver of the skin and 'twist' it over the prepared drink releasing the fruit's essential oils over the surface. Drop the twist into drink. This gives the cocktail another dimension in flavour as well as being aesthetically pleasing.

PHOTO CREDITS

Original cover image: © John Ross (image manipulation by Warren Bonett, p 2 Photo by Adrian Wilson, courtesy of Meena Khera PR; pp 6-7, 110-12, 115 Courtesy of The Setai; pp 8, 32, 66(t), 77, 109 Courtesy of Alessi SpA, www.alessi.com; p 9 The Art Archive/Dagli Orti; p 10 The Art Archive/Gift of Mrs Claire Lewis/Museum of the City of NewYork/91.102.2.1; pp 11, 74-5 Courtesy of Morgans Hotel Group; pp 12(l); 130-1, 133 Courtesy of The Blue Bar, The Berkeley; p 12(r) Courtesy of The Savoy; p 13 Columbia/The Kobal Collection; pp 14, 94-7, 99 © Photo by Alberto Ferrero; pp 16-8, 21 Photo by Amit Pasricha, courtesy of Conran & Partners; p 19 © Paul Cowan; pp 20, 25(l), 26, 36, 44, 48, 60, 67, 71, 83, 93, 98, 119, 129, 150, 160-3 Courtesy of Bombay Sapphire; pp 22-4, 25(r), 27 Courtesy of TMSK; pp 28-31, 33 Courtesy of Sketch; pp 34-5, 37-9 Courtesy of Frisson; pp 40-1, 43, 45 Courtesy of Food Scope NY, LLC; p 42 Images from John Gauntner, *The Saké Companion – A Connoisseur's Guide*, Running Press (Pennsylvania), 2000; pp 46-7, 49, 51 © One Aldwych Hotel, www.onealdwych.com; p 50 MGM/The Kobal Collection; pp 52-5 Courtesy of the Scarlet; pp 56-8, 61 © Rafael Vargas; p 59 Courtesy of Stelton A/S, www.stelton.com; pp 62-5, 66(b) Courtesy of The Merivale Group; pp 68-70, 72(b), 73 Courtesy of Semiramis Athens/design hotels™ www.designhotels.com; p 72(t) Courtesy of www.copco.com; p 76 Morley Von Sternberg/Arcaid; pp 78-9, 80(b), 82 Photo by Koji Okamura courtesy of Conran & Partners; p 80(t) Courtesy of Terence Conran Ltd; p 81 Photo by Jamie Abbott courtesy of Terence Conran Ltd; pp 84-5, 87 Hotel Q!/Dirk Schaper; p 86 © Photo by Dominik Gigler, www.gigler.com; pp 88-90, 92 © Doug Snower Photography; p 91 © Jordan Mozer; pp 100-2, 103(r), 104-5 Courtesy of Hakkasan Group; pp 106-7 Courtesy of design hotels™ www.designhotels.com; p 108 © Anna Chelnokova; pp 113, 118 Warner Bros/The Kobal Collection; p 114 © Sandra O'Claire; pp 116-7 Courtesy of Momo Restaurant Familial; pp 120-2 Courtesy of Zark Fatah; p 123 Photo by Volker Seding; pp 124-5, 127-8 Courtesy of Murano Urban Resort; p 126 © Matt Glenovich; p 132 © Photo by Rick Guest; pp 134-5, 139 Courtesy of www.hospitalityholdings.com; p 136 © Rebecca Ellis; p 137 20th Century Fox/The Kobal Collection; p 138 © Photo by Jill DeGroff; pp 140-3 © Nakasa and Partners; pp 144-6 Photo by Jordi Cuixart, courtesy of Hotel Omm; p 147 The Kobal Collection; pp 148-9, 153 Photo by Russell Baer; p 151 Courtesy of Treehouse PR; p 152 Doug Liman/Miramax/The Kobal Collection; pp 154-5, 157, 159 Photos by Shania Shegedyn; p 156 MGM/Eon/The Kobal Collection/Hamshere, Keith; p 158 © Photo by Abi Wyles

TOGETHER FOREVER

RUN-DMC

BEASTIE BOYS

GLEN E. FRIEDMAN

TOGETHER FOREVER

RIZZOLI

NEW YORK

New York · Paris · London · Milan

FOREWORD BY **CHRIS ROCK**

My introduction to rap music was when I first heard, and then saw this guy walking down the street with a huge JVC, pulsating equalizer, boom box, blasting a tape of Grand Wizard Theodore freestyling at the Hotel Diplomat over the beat of "Funky Penguin." I thought to myself, "What the fuck was that?" That's when I first discovered rap and what we called "gangster tapes." Not long after that, it was all about getting new "gangster tapes" from the Bronx—"Let's get the tapes, let's go to the Bronx."

My friends and I were inspired and excited. We were like DJ groupies, watching the technique of guys like Grandmaster Flash and others. We just marveled at what they were doing and I became obsessed with DJs even before rap.

Truth be told, I was a DJ way before I told jokes. Run-DMC's "Sucker MC's" taught me a lot about controlling the audience. I learned things about control and timing from playing that record at block parties that I use to this day. That record would start a fight in the right circumstance, you had to be careful how you played it! I witnessed people getting beat the fuck down to "Sucker MC's"!

That song made a real impression on me. It was raw like nothing I had ever heard before; Jam Master Jay's scratching was more instrumental than any I had heard before it on a record—it was thrilling. Run's opening verse was cool, but when DMC took the mic, I was all about it. It was the greatest thing I ever heard.

I probably first noticed Beastie Boys when they came to my ear on the *Krush Groove* movie soundtrack. (Side note: My first ever appearance in a major film was as an extra in *Krush Groove*. I was in the scene where Blair Underwood, playing Russell, fights his brother Run.) The song was "She's On It!" I really liked it, but once *Licensed to Ill* came out, I was in love. It wasn't only because of obviously great tracks like "Slow and Low" and "It's The New Style." My comedy friends and I really liked "Girls," too. We would listen to it over and over and over. They were really funny! If they grew up on a different block, they would have become comedians instead of rappers. I really believe that. Depending on how you want to look at it, they grew up on either the right or wrong block.

People always get caught up in what these two iconic groups stood for, but can we just step back for a moment and say, who gives a fuck?

They were good!

They made amazing records!

Run, D., Yauch, Ad-Rock, and Mike D are all GREAT MCs. That's what they do. Voices, styles, and rhymes: hard to beat. Let's just get that outta the way. And how's this for a little bit of flavor: Run-DMC and Beastie Boys made us all believe we never had to dress up again, for anything. They came out on stage in their street clothes before anyone else in the genre—they introduced sneakers as legitimate shoes.

Rap music is the first art form created by "free" black people. Yes, black people invented rock 'n' roll, the blues, and jazz, but those were all basically created by slaves or people living a slave-like existence. I picked up on the freedom of Run-DMC. They helped me to understand and gave me pride to feel that we don't have to act in any way different for anybody; we could truly be ourselves all the time, no matter who was around. Before experiencing their music, I remember when I would go places with family where when there were people of other races around we had to "act" differently. Assimilating was important to the elders, but Run-DMC, and Beastie Boys too for that matter, gave us the inspiration and the attitude to really say "The hell with all this acting proper bullshit." The attitude I got from them was liberating. It was inspirational.

Rap was the opposite of Martin Luther King; it wasn't about integration. It's really about our own thing, and fuck what the world wanted from us. We became our own. Rap parallels punk rock: Destroy everything that came before it and borrow little bits to help you get there. Bring it full circle: it helps us understand how and why these two groups did what they did, and why Glen E. brings us into the picture deeper than anyone and brings it all together. Forever. These photographs inspire and excite us to this day.

RUN DMC — CHRISTMAS IN HOLLIS / PETER PIPER

WALK THIS WAY — RUN DMC — 12" SINGLE

IT'S TRICKY (AND MORE)

SPECIALLY PRICED 6-TRACK EP

BEASTIE BOYS — NO SLEEP TILL BROOKLYN

BEASTIE BOYS — CHECK YOUR HEAD

beastie boys ..intergalactic..

Let's give all these photographs some context. I had a bit of a long-distance teenage romance with a girl named Arabella Field, who actually introduced me to Adam Yauch (her childhood and lifelong friend) as well as Michael Diamond, outside of CBGB's one day after they opened for Bad Brains in the summer of 1981. Yauch had his skateboard, a Powell board if memory serves me, and he kinda knew who I was from *SkateBoarder* magazine, but those kids could never 'fess up to anything as uncool as recognizing someone they had not met already. Mike was just the kinda awkward singer and a "close talker" that our mutual friend convinced me to give a ride home one evening, possibly that one after the hardcore matinee, in the Rent-A-Wreck I was driving packed with friends while visiting my dad on the east coast. I dropped Mike just off the Harlem River Drive, by his street, but unfortunately for him, the wrong side of Manhattan—he lived on Central Park West, so the ride I gave him didn't help that much. He reminded me of that the next few times I met up with him (sorry Mike). I saw Beastie Boys playing that day for just a song or two, they actually threw marshmallows at the audience, poking fun at the "hardcore" kids . . . I didn't like that, or their music too much. I went back outside just to hang with friends; I did not make any pictures of them at all.

In the following summer of 1982, I was in the city visiting as I usually did in the summer. Arabella told me there was to be a screening of the Sex Pistols film *The Great Rock 'n' Roll Swindle* at a roller rink early in the evening before they were open for disco roller skating for the movie's U.S. and New York City premiere. The rink was on the west side around 18th street & 10th avenue, and was called The Roxy. After we watched the movie, all of us sitting on the floor around a 24-inch TV set, we were just about to leave when we noticed Yauch was there. He told us we might want to stick around. These kids called the Rock Steady Crew were gonna be practicing in the middle of the floor, b-boying, breaking. I had no idea what he was talking about, but he convinced me to stay. As these guys gathered around in a circle with each of them dancing one at a time in the center of this small circle, in the center of the floor, where people were slowly filling in the perimeter, roller skating to the music, we stood just outside of their circle, just a few of us. These kids were going off, and my mind was blown. I asked the obvious leader, the main kid of the crew, Crazy Legs, if any of them skated; it seemed to me like someone had to be down with skateboarding if they were doing this shit. He said yeah, "I think he does" and pointed to one of his crew—a young "Doze" Green. I wanted to photograph this one day. Ideas and concepts started spinning in my head—but that's another story. Thanks to Yauch, I saw the Rock Steady Crew in an intimate setting the same summer I saw Minor Threat play at the 9:30 Club in Washington, D.C. Both events were life-altering and inspirational beyond words I could conjure up here.

Back cover of Beastie Boys' first record, and the friend who shot that photo, Arabella.

Photo: Dave Parsons

A few months later I was back in L.A. and Arabella sent me some early hip-hop mix tapes she had made for me from dubs and records she had picked up, besides the obvious Sugar Hill Gang, There was the Treacherous Three doing "The New Rap Language," among others, and the real standout to me was The Funky Four Plus One's "It's the Joint." Hip-hop was making a deep impression on me. I was beginning to see it as black kids' version of punk rock in spirit. Around the same time Mike sent me their first 7" EP *Pollywog Stew*, Arabella did the group photo on the back, and he autographed it, which I thought was odd for a punk rock kid.

Run-DMC's song "Sucker MC's" changed hip-hop forever, but "Jam Master Jay" was the one I heard toward the end of my stint running the Suicidal Tendencies show (I got their record deal, produced the album, and did all the photography of course). That song made me think "I'm gonna get into this, this hip-hop stuff, I'm gonna get down with this shit one day soon, I have no idea how, but it's gonna happen." It was dynamic, hard, innovative, and inspiring, as much as the documentary *Style Wars* was earlier that same year.

Fast forward just six months or so: I quit managing the band Suicidal, shook hands, and said good luck (motherfuckers)! I was still making skateboarding photographs on occasion and shooting at punk gigs too, but both were waning in interest for me, both getting a bit generic and no longer the inspiration they once were to me personally. I was in school at UCLA and that was a bit disappointing too; I became disillusioned with college. I had been published since I was fourteen, put out my own "fanzine" at twenty that sold more than any other 'zine in the genre up to that point, and had produced

an album that was playing on the most popular radio station in southern California, as well as a video in rotation on MTV that I was responsible for. And UCLA didn't think my grades were up to snuff to allow me into the Communications program I wanted to be a part of. So I started taking classes that sounded interesting and didn't think of what I needed to take to graduate. I don't even know if I ever declared a major, but political philosophy courses was where I ended up most. I continued at school for a while longer.

I had heard the Beasties made a rap record, it was kind of a goof, but it was really funny (as usual). Then I heard they were coming out west on Madonna's first ever nationwide tour to support her album *Like A Virgin*; they were to be the opening act for MTV's newest, brightest Lucky Star. One of the guys called me before they got out to see if I could hang and show them around. The timing could not have been better: school was slow and I was trying to get away from my own "Rock 'n' Roll Swindle." I met up with them as soon as they

got in town and from that moment on it was laughter and belligerence every step of the way. I was inspired by where they were going with hip-hop. I really wanted to help, and make great photographs for them.

But business first, at least according to their management company. They needed a photo of them with Madonna for publicity purposes—problem was, Madonna was so insecure with her new fame that she wouldn't even pose with her opening act. When she asked me why I wanted to get a picture of her with the boys, I replied "because we want to make them as famous as you." Her reply: "That's not very funny!" She wouldn't pose with them, so I had another idea to make the publicists happy: we went into the audience and shot photos of the group with her performing in the background! Unfortunately, no one liked that idea as much as we did—but the ball was rolling!

I got them an interview on Rodney Bingenheimer's KROQ radio show live while Madonna was performing in the background. Rodney hated rap and refused to play the few rap singles they had out, but he did alternate songs from the punk *Pollywog Stew* EP and Madonna's *Like A Virgin* album. It was hilarious, and this was still at an early point before their fame. At Madonna's shows the Beasties were practically booed off stage most nights. After the shows there were crazy numbers of celebrities hanging around backstage, and we started taking photos with any of the ones we recognized, just for fun.

They had rented a huge Lincoln Continental Town Car and either Yauch or I usually drove (I'm sure Mike didn't have a license and of course 'Vitz probably wasn't even old enough to have a driver's license). We had AC/DC or Black Sabbath BLASTING from the car stereo with all the windows rolled down, as we pulled up to the venue where Madonna was going to be presented with her first-ever gold record for the sale of her first 500,000 albums. There was a small driveway where the valet would take the car; Adam pulls in way over the normal speed limit and skids loudly to a halt, and we all fling the doors open like we own the place, when clearly NO ONE gave a shit that this Beastie crew showed up. Music still blasting, we leave the car and go inside. The party was the usual Hollywood fare: celebrities wall-to-wall, big multi-flavored popcorn dispensers, the works. We're all having a good time, and on occasion one of the guys grab me to take another photo of them with another new celebrity friend. Finally, the big moment arrives: Madonna is about to be presented with her plaque from the head of Sire records, Seymour Stein—the same label that released

debut LPs from The Ramones and The Dead Boys, to name a few—it's HER gold record party, Sean Penn is courting her, and she wouldn't even let the paparazzi get a photo of her with the plaque and Seymour. She covered her face with the plaque! Maybe she had a pimple or something; but her insecurity in that moment shone brightly. Or maybe she was just tired of being exploited now that she was clearly able to take hold of the reins herself?

Over these three days or so the Boys were in town, I was part tour guide, friend they knew from the punk era, and even part-time manager—easy for me to slide into that part, because I had just stopped that role for ST not that long before. I even had Russell's (Simmons) all-access pass for the first few nights I was there, because neither he nor Rick were around anywhere; just their "road manager" producer/friend/temporary DJ Scott Jarvis was looking after them when they were at their hotels or the venues. Otherwise it was a free-for-all.

Because I was so excited by this new sound of the time and my punk friends were a part of it, I was inspired to make real photos with them, beyond the goofing-with-celebrities. We started doing portraits all over the place—whenever I came up with an idea or a place to shoot, they were game. I took them down to the coolest college radio station in Los Angeles, KXLU, for an interview and made lots of great photos on the Loyola campus afterward. I introduced them to the fish-eye lens, which they fell in love with and used to their massive advantage for years to come, both with and without me behind the lens—I never minded when they used it on their own, but when others bit it was annoying. This was the same fish-eye lens I had made some of my most iconic skateboarding photos with. The Beasties' creativity and humor helped to inspire some of the great photos that we created over those days—we made a lot of incredible stuff. I also brought them to Fat Burger and Tommy's Chili burger for their first time, contrary to how they remember it and wrote in their own book. I was still a year-and-a-half from becoming vegan, so back then I was all in! And I can't forget to mention: hanging with these three was a nonstop laughfest. They would have me literally crying with laughter every day; it was almost like a game: who can be the first to make Glen laugh 'til he cries.

When I initially sent the proof sheets or test prints back to New York for Russell and Rick to look over, they all freaked out. They had never seen such a bounty

of great images from one session and they didn't even know what to do with them all, with the exception of the goof paparazzi shots. We negotiated a usage fee for a bunch of them; I was charging $400 and they had never paid that much before for a session, let alone one they couldn't own, but they had no choice. I had the goods and they had to pay; besides, they had never even dreamed photos could be this good. It was the beginning of a lifelong relationship with Russell and his Rush Productions management, and Rick and Def Jam Recordings.

A few months later Run-DMC was coming to L.A. to tape an episode of Dick Clark's *American Bandstand*. Rick and Russell asked if I could go hang out, show the two of them around too, and do some photos of Run-DMC, in addition to getting the requisite pictures with Dick Clark on set. Rick had known my work from the punk rock era—Black Flag, Minor Threat, Bad Brains, etc.—and Russell didn't know me from shit, except from those dope Beastie photos we made when they were in L.A. We met, and almost instantly Rick, Russell, and I were thick as thieves. We shared an intense love of the music, and were all over-the-top enthusiastic about things we loved, and a lot of those things were similar. After the *American Bandstand* taping I was given the opportunity to make pictures with Run, D, and Jay outside of their hotel in the Wilshire district, and then some scattered appearances performing around town, sometimes in front of thousands of people, and sometimes in front of only a few.

I honestly can't remember all the different situations and when they happened, but there's lots of photo evidence we got that proved we could work well together. I was really stoked to be working with these guys and we were all within a few years of each other in age, so we got along well. I saw them as stars in a new world of music. I had never really worked with any music groups who stayed in hotels—usually it was bands on floors while on the road—and nobody but fanzines ever wanted to use the music photography I was making, other than when

I pushed *SkateBoarder* and *Action Now* to publish and talk about the stuff I was into. But suddenly the stuff I was shooting was hot, and everyone wanted in. Most of the photography in the culture up to that point was pretty basic and usually studio-driven (read: boring and whack). Images of music groups out in the real world were usually low in quality. I did what I could to remedy this, because the culture and the artists deserved it! These groups inspired me and I wanted to spread that inspiration around— frame it, compose it, beautify it, create great work to inspire and teach others who didn't know about it and what the fuck was up. Attitude, culture, change.

Within two or three visits Run, D, and Jay wanted no one but me to make their photographs. They flew me out to NYC to come make photos for their upcoming tour

Rick, Dick Clark, ill Badler (publicist), Run, Russell, D, and Jay, at *American Bandstand* '85

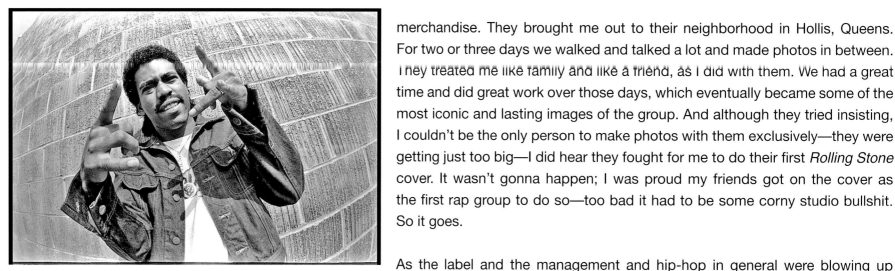

merchandise. They brought me out to their neighborhood in Hollis, Queens. For two or three days we walked and talked a lot and made photos in between. They treated me like family and like a friend, as I did with them. We had a great time and did great work over those days, which eventually became some of the most iconic and lasting images of the group. And although they tried insisting, I couldn't be the only person to make photos with them exclusively—they were getting just too big—I did hear they fought for me to do their first *Rolling Stone* cover. It wasn't gonna happen; I was proud my friends got on the cover as the first rap group to do so—too bad it had to be some corny studio bullshit. So it goes.

As the label and the management and hip-hop in general were blowing up like nothing I had ever worked with before, I was helping out Russell and Rick with many of the groups when they came to L.A.; not always making photos but often helping with promotion, radio play, and press, and just showing people around; driving in my classic 1971 dark green Mercedes Benz 280 SEL that I had just bought used (I even let JMJ borrow it once, and I never let anyone borrow my car!). I got Kurtis Blow on some local radio, promoted a show where the infamous music industry leader Andre Harell performed, and killed it as part of his group Dr. Jekyll and Mr. Hyde! I was even offered the job of being LL Cool J's road manager early on. I had some incredible fun being referred to as Def Jam's west coast representative—which really meant nothing as far as real employment or salary—way before they actually had the "Def Jam West" label. I was still in school at UCLA most days of the week, but I was traveling east to work with Russell and Rick in New York City a lot.

On one trip I was with Run-DMC traveling up and down the west coast, rarely making photos; just hanging out and helping and being part of the entourage on this fun ride. I mention this specifically because when we went up to Oakland for Run-DMC to play at the Coliseum I witnessed probably the greatest hip-hop performance of my life. It was a huge basketball arena and the place was packed to the rafters, literally. As soon as they hit the stage the place was going completely out of their minds, I swear every person from the first row to the very last up in the nosebleed section was singing and dancing along with every lyric spoken. I was just there soaking it all in without a camera in between my face and the performance—sorry.

Later that year or the maybe the next, the *Raising Hell* tour came to Madison Square Garden, and it was arguably the most important hip-hop show of the era.

Kurtis Blow, Hollywood, 1986 and LL Cool J, UCLA, 1986

Beastie Boys and Boogie Down Productions were also on the bill, timely and slamming. When Jay dropped the needle on "My Adidas," Run and D pointed at their shoes and told everyone in the audience to show theirs. Thousands of shoes and sweat suits were held up all around. Angelo and Raquel were two "Hollywood" reps for Adidas who attended the show, and after seeing the impact and the fan loyalty on display, they offered Run-DMC the first-ever brand endorsement deal with a non-athlete. At the time it was unheard of; the deal was for a million dollars. Kids from Queens just wearing what they did every day, having their say. I met Chuckie D.—later known as Chuck D of Public Enemy—for the first time at that MSG show as well. He was smaller in person than I had imagined him to be; after Rick played me his phenomenal demos, I thought a guy with that voice was gonna be 6'4" and 250 lbs!

When I came back in the fall to shoot stills on the movie set for *Tougher Than Leather* for Adidas over a period of two weeks, I kind of realized I was always a New Yorker at heart, and soon after that shoot and at the urging of Rick and Russell I moved back to the city permanently. It took me a little over a year before I got my own place, but between using Russell's village apartment while he was out on the road most days of the week and my dad's couch across the bridge in Fort Lee, NJ, it was undoubtedly the place to be for me. I was hyper-inspired by all that was going on at the time, and I was making record covers mostly for Def Jam, but others too.

When the Beasties' first album hit, shit began to get a little crazy. That bullshit "(You Gotta) Fight For Your Right (To Party)" surprised the hell out of us and blew them up. In December right before it went INSANE, I was asked to shoot a cover for *Spin* magazine. We walked all over downtown for the session that day, making classic photos by the Washington Square arch; in Chelsea at the old Sloan's supermarket where we just walked in and started shooting; near Laguardia Place across from Russell's four-floor walk-up where I was staying; and last stop in front of the Def Jam Rush office at 298 Elizabeth Street, where we made the cover photo for *Spin*, and other better ones they didn't pick!

I worked with both groups many times over the years and hung out with them without making photos many more times. In the early days I prided myself giving political talks and ear-opening music to Run-DMC. It was mostly just filling in holes about things they might have heard only a little about in their world, like explaining the real-life practical differences in political parties to Joey or showing him how apartheid in South Africa

Anti-apartheid Punk educational pamphlet shared with Run.

Album cover designs for *Ill Communication* (1994) and *Tougher Than Leather* (1988) that the public never got to see.

really affected the people there (because even though he had already performed at an antiapartheid rally in the mid-'80s he wasn't really clear what it was) or turning Jay on to the Bad Brains and Minor Threat. I used to get the Beasties hooked up with skate gear before they were world-famous; you can see Yauch wearing lots of skate shirts in their videos and live show pictures that I had gotten for him during the early years.

Before Run-DMC's record label ever had made a picture-sleeve 12-inch single, they came to me asking for my photo to be on the very first one they would do, for the single "Walk This Way." I loved Aerosmith in the mid '70s as a little skate rat, so I had to be down with this. They knew that, and took advantage of me, the cheap bastards—they offered me $100 and said "if you don't give us the photograph we'll just stick to our generic sleeve." DAMN. Fuck it, it was gonna be important, so I did it. I told Joey the story later in the day at the Rush office and he took the knot out of his pocket and peeled off four $100 bills and said "thank you Glen, I hope this helps." We once did comps for a Run-DMC LP cover for *Tougher Than Leather*; it was a hundred times better than the one they went with, but I wasn't going to let the label rip me off and the band understood. The label wanted to own everything. I don't roll like that EVER, so we never had a LP cover together. The label said the record-buying public can barely recognize the difference between a decent and a great cover anyway. So, in other words: it wasn't worth it to them to do business fairly when they could just exploit a young up-and-comer or desperate old-timer behind the camera. Fuck that. But we did make pictures for a couple of other singles, and after that first bullshit with "Walk This Way" and the undeniable success the record company had with it, I think I got closer to my normal rate for the "It's Tricky!" 12-inch and a Euro sleeve for the "Christmas in Hollis" single.

New York and the world were going off, hip-hop as a culture was having a major impact everywhere. It was hard to believe and we were all in the center of it—all the groups, not just these two but the entire Rush roster was groundbreaking and setting the pace for what defined hip-hop and its immense success on all fronts.

One of my most inspiring visits with Mike and the two Adams was a few years later, when I was out in LA to visit my mom for Thanksgiving. I had seen Adam in NYC by chance a month earlier and he told me to give them a call and come visit their new studio and base of operations on my next trip west. I hadn't seen them since they moved out west to join up with new management and Capitol Records after everything on the *Licensed to Ill* tour soured for them with Def Jam and Rush. So after the holiday meal I gave Adam a call and he invited me to come up to the "G-Spot" in Atwater Village—a place in L.A. I had never even heard of 'til they put it on my map. It was all laughs as I saw them and they showed me around the studio and the live room that included a skate ramp that Yauch was particularly proud to show me, and the basketball hoop bolted to the wall just over the recording booth. We played some ball and they offered to play me some recent tracks they had recorded for their next album. They had not yet sequenced it and still were not 100% about which songs would even make the cut. We listened and shot hoops. I was fucked-up-crazy-impressed, and totally inspired by what I was hearing!

The *Paul's Boutique* LP was incredible, but THIS was AMAZING. I loved it, and I was super-excited that they were playing their own instruments again as well! Before the end of the night I asked them if they had an album cover done yet. Much to my dismay they said "yeah, it's done." I replied "Well let's go make some photos anyway, I am loving this, I want to make some great photos with y'all, it's been a few years, let's do something! I'm flying back to NYC soon but let's get together before I get on the red-eye Monday night and meet in the morning and shoot as long as it feels good."

We met by the Capitol Records building on Franklin by Vine in Hollywood at around 10 am. Yauch had a concept in mind: he really wanted to see if I could make a photo with them that felt similar to the photo I had made with Minor Threat for their last record. We talked about that idea and a few others. The obvious way to replicate the *Salad Days* cover was to shoot the group up at Yauch's log cabin on Lookout Mountain Road. But before we worked on that concept, I had them humor me with an idea that I had discussed with them at the studio: I wanted them to bring their instrument cases, and Mike would just have a brown paper bag with his drum sticks and a microphone. I wanted to create an image of them similar to how I remembered seeing kids in bands walking down a street on their way to a practice space in New York City.

Minor Threat *Salad Days,* 1983 photograph that Yauch wanted to emulate, and our more obvious attempt.

We shot one roll not far from where we parked. After I made the last three images on the roll, I knew I had what Adam was looking for—it wasn't the porch shot, but it had the same integrity and feel.

I had my good friend and former Suicidal Tendencies drummer, Amery Smith, drive us all around in his van for the day. The boys brought their cases and a change of clothes or two and left their cars there. We went to the log cabin, up to Wonderland School, then to Runyon Canyon, and ended up down at the beach in Santa Monica and across the street on the cliff side of the Pacific Coast Highway, too. Parked in the lot by an empty pool I used to shoot pictures of the DogTown guys in back in 1977. The day ended, the sun had set by the time we got the crew back to their cars—we had a blast. Mike got to talking a bit with Amery about drumming and a few months later called me for Amery's number; he asked him to join their band! Yeah "AWOL," that's Amery.

I got on a plane that night, brought the film to the lab, and a few days later made some prints and faxed copies of them to Mike. I knew we had some good stuff. Turns out they all agreed the last image we made of them sitting on the curb with their cases and the brown paper bag was what I thought it was going to be. I was told they abandoned their earlier cover design and image, and loved the faxed image so much they told the designer to put it on the *Check Your Head* LP cover as was. Typical Beastie Boys shit, I had to laugh it off and was just happy I was able to contribute to this great album.

Over the years, the trials and tribulations of superstardom can affect people in different ways. The photographs in this book, through it all, tell part of the story of these two groups who shared a lot, more than most and held it together better than most. We shared a lot and were friends, but honestly, once I take the camera out, work is getting done!

Run-DMC were doing a video for the song "What's It All About" I produced along with Jam Master Jay in 1990. I pushed for them to get a little political, and to use the Stone Roses' "Fool's Gold" bass-line over James Brown's "Funky Drummer," but the song took a "New Jack Swing" turn, not to mention Joey adding the Johnny Mathis sample for the chorus, and the combo kinda doomed it for my ear. I still had brought my camera down to the shoot figuring there may be some moments under the bridge that would compel me to make some photographs. They're not my favorites, but some are interesting, and they were the last I made with them as a group.

When the Beasties finished their fifth album in NYC in 1998, they invited a bunch of friends down for an informal listening party in the studio. I had just got back from my *Fuck You All* exhibition in Sydney, Australia, and had yet to finish the roll of B&W film I had started a year earlier in London where I had photographed the *Fuck You All* rooms at the Institute of Contemporary Art. With pictures from both of these great exhibitions and even a few skate shots taken on a ramp out on Bondi Beach still waiting to be processed, I decided to bring my camera down to the listening party so I could finally finish the roll! Only problem: Mike wasn't there when I walked in. I learned that earlier that day he got elbowed in the eye during a basketball game. Eventually he showed up with a huge bandage across his face. I said "Damn Mike, what the fuck? You OK?" He was. For a laugh we decided to make some photos using the last of that roll that had seen exposures on three continents by the end of this evening, and they used one of those photos on the "Intergalactic" 10-inch vinyl single and also used it for publicity. That might have been the last time we made group photos.

Run-DMC and Beastie Boys are some incredibly talented individuals. We didn't always get along perfectly, that's what often happens with creative types, you bump heads on occasion. 'Vitz even mentioned to me once after Adam had passed: "You guys both had intense visions and were perfectionists, hard to make that work all the time . . . ." But the mutual respect was and has always been there.

In addition to the countless magazine pages, promo photos, various record sleeves worldwide, merchandise posters, world tour books, calendars, and T-shirts we did with my photos over the years, I produced that Run-DMC song with Jam Master Jay, wrote articles for the Beasties' *Grand Royal* magazine, went to a few weddings, even made newlywed pictures a couple of times, wrote a letter to an advisory board to help with an adoption, yelled back-up vocals on the song "Run's House" (recorded at at Jimi Hendrix's Electric Lady Studios), appeared for a moment in the beginning of the "(You Gotta) Fight for Your Right (To Party!)" video, advised and critiqued all these good friends on different things over the years, and still play softball every season with Horovitz.

Together Forever.

GEF

Above: Pass for the August 17, 1986 Long Beach arena show, notorious last of the era, due to fear of gang violence.

Corral Beach, Malibu, CA, 1985

Oasis Church, Wilshire District, Los Angeles, CA, 1985

Hotel fire escape, Wilshire District, Los Angeles, CA, 1985

Elizabeth Street, New York, 1986

Fresh Fest II, Los Angeles Memorial Sports Arena, 1985

Russell being thrown a bribe from Bernie (played by Richard Edson), in the movie *Tougher Than Leather*, 1986

Run-DMC and Beastie Boys were two rebel bands

who forged their own unique sounds without regard for the climate of rap records or any of the music that was popular at the time when they came along. I think this was at least partly because they were not being managed or produced by traditional commercial minds, and therefore they were not influenced by "the norm." They were not just rappers who spit rhymes over commercial tracks. They were encouraged to be the individuals that they became. Part of their genius was simply their insistence on having the freedom to follow their own and the streets' inspiration. The fact that they were more interested in exciting their core fans and themselves with their art rather than the general market was precisely why they grew to the iconic status they reside in still.

During the time they all toured together something significant was going on, beyond the entertainment and fun. Still innocents, I believe even they may have missed what a sociological phenomenon they were. Run–DMC–JMJ and Beastie Boys united fans and helped to change the way millions of teenagers viewed race, viewed themselves, and viewed the world.

RUSSELL SIMMONS

197 & Hollis Ave., D's block. Hollis, Queens, New York, 1985

Opening for Madonna, Universal Amphitheatre, Los Angeles, CA, April 1985

First-ever rap group to appear on *American Bandstand*

Opening night for Krush Groove at one of the biggest theaters in Los Angeles, October 25, 1985

Public appearance in South Central Los Angeles, CA, 1985

After a live broadcast on KXLU radio, Loyola Marymount University, Los Angeles, CA, 1985

When Beastie Boys were still a guitar-based punk band, there weren't very many rap groups.

No such thing as a big rap group. But Run-DMC were among the most cutting-edge and respected ones to us.

We really looked up to Run-DMC. I'm saying "we," because I DJ'ed for the Beasties at the time. Hip-hop before Run-DMC was carrying the baggage of R&B music. But Run-DMC didn't embrace R&B or look like an R&B band. They stepped outside of the continuing lineage and became one of the first real b-boy artists. Part of the rap, graffiti, and breakdance cultures that were happening. Yet at the same time they were street-level rock 'n' roll.

When our relationship with them started, we got to hang out with the group we most looked up to. Run-DMC got to hang out with these punk kids who came from a different world than they did.

We both shared a sort of outsider experience. Run-DMC were outsiders from mainstream culture. The Beasties were outsiders from hip-hop culture.

Being accepted by Run-DMC and touring with Run-DMC was a mark of authenticity for Beastie Boys. There was a feeling of family between the two groups. Together we were a unified movement working to move forward this culture.

This hip-hop music that nobody else seemed to care about but us and our friends. There was tremendous passion, energy, and hard work, and a shared humor put into it. Hip-hop was so new that it could have gone in any direction at that time. Had it been rooted in jazz music, it could have gone in the that direction instead and been really good as well—it just happened to move forward with the cast of characters and the experiences we had growing up.

I was seeing the purity of hip-hop through a filter of punk rock and hard rock. And that worked its way into the music.

Success was never the aim, but it eventually came in a way none of us ever could have imagined. When we started hearing songs we'd worked on together on the radio and when Run-DMC headlined Madison Square Garden, I was in my college dorm room thinking, "This is unbelievable."

It wasn't the attention that was unbelievable—what was unbelievable was that people actually liked the crazy music we were making.

RICK RUBIN

On the corner of
Broadway and Houston,
SoHo, New York, 1987

Hollywood Palladium, Los Angeles, CA, 1985

"Jamaica Park" aka Haggerty Park, Hollis, Queens, New York, 1985

Hollis Presbyterian Church, Hollis, Queens, New York, 1985

LaGuardia Place, Greenwich Village, New York, 1986

Los Angeles street scene, free concert in front of City Hall, Los Angeles, CA, 1985

Washington Square Park, Greenwich Village, New York, 1986

"The Buildings" at 196 & Hollis, Queens, New York, 1985

"The Castle"
aka Blair House, 195 & Woodhull, Hollis, Queens, New York

Sloan's Market, Chelsea, New York, 1986

Beastie Boys are brilliant!

I love them because they were a punk band that also had the desire to do hip-hop, and they did it above and beyond all expectations!

They created great songs, and great music with funny, outrageous, amusing lyrics. And in my humble opinion, they are one of the best live shows in music history.

As the music form progressed, so did they.

The consciousness they gained over time can be seen as a lesson for all.

They were, and still are, an inspiration to me.

Besides, I could never forget that their dedication to hip-hop was real—these dudes knew more about Busy Bee and Spoonie Gee than me!

I remember when they first came into the studio with us, Rick asked Jay, "Do you think these guys could make a hip-hop song?" Jay replied, "Hell yeah, they already have fucking hip-hop attitude!"

As Jam Master Jay would say, "Ain't no one cooler than Beastie Boys, period."

DARRYL "DMC" MCDANIELS

Raising Hell tour, 1986

Live at the Ritz, NYC, 1986

Live a the Capitol Theatre, Passaic, NJ, 1987

Live 1986–1987

August 17,1987 with Vanessa Williams backstage at the infamous
Raising Hell Long Beach Arena show shortly after her Miss
America resignation

With opening act Public Enemy backstage at the Capitol Theatre
at the start of the *Licensed To Ill* tour, 1987

With Gene Simmons of KISS after Madonna's *Like A Virgin* show, 1985

With Joey Ramone backstage at the New York Music Awards, Beacon Theatre, New York, 1985

With Billy Idol after Madonna's *Like A Virgin* show, 1985

With Dick Clark on the set of *American Bandstand*, 1985

With "Weird Al" Yankovic at Madonna's *Like A Virgin* Gold Record party, The Islander, West Hollywood, CA, 1985

With Rob Lowe at Madonna's *Like A Virgin* show, 1985

With Lou Rawls at the *Lou Rawls Parade of Stars Telethon*, a benefit for The United Negro College Fund, Hollywood, CA, 1985

"I was so hammered here; I thought I was taking a pic with Josie & The Pussycats..." —David Lee Roth

With David Lee Roth and Sean Penn at Madonna's *Like A Virgin* Gold Record party, The Islander, West Hollywood, CA, 1985

With Toni Basil after Madonna's *Like A Virgin* show, 1985

With Judd Nelson at Madonna's *Like A Virgin*
Gold Record party, The Islander, West Hollywood, CA, 1985

With George Clinton backstage at the New York
Music Awards, Beacon Theatre, New York, 1985

"Iron" Mike Tyson joins Beastie Boys onstage at the Hollywood Bowl, *Together Forever* tour, 1987

Hollis Crew backstage party with Adidas reps, Raquel and Angelo, after the show

Jam Master Jay and DMC receiving their solid gold shell toe pendants

Adidas in the air at Madison Square Garden, 1986

In the summer of 1986, Beastie Boys opened for RUN-DMC on their *Raising Hell* tour.

Every night, when they performed, me, Adam, and Mike would be on the side of the stage, studying their every move and word. It was probably the first time I'd ever paid attention in school. They were the combination of what makes artistic energy happen.

Pyramid power, if you will.

Run was the crazy artist type who just did not do things the normal way. Always manic and moving.

DMC was the quiet comic book nerd who also was menacing looking enough to have been cast in the role of *My Bodyguard*.

And Jam Master Jay was the conductor. He was the supercool one in the band. You'd look to Jay to know how to dress, and talk, and walk, and carry yourself with confidence.

Besides Simon and Garfunkel and The Ramones, no other kids from Queens rocked to so many people.

So Jay orchestrated how a rap group should perform in an arena. He'd set the tempo, and Run would take command. They'd put on their trademark felt fedoras and transform into superheroes.

They were the sound of the future stripped down to its origins. Drums and voices.

A Run-DMC performance was like a class in session: they taught us that if you can rock a stage, then you can rock the world.

ADAM HOROVITZ

Santa Monica Pier,
CA, 1985

"A Day of Peace" with Barry White; an anti-gang violence day hosted by radio station KDAY, Los Angeles, CA, 1986

On the set of *Tougher Than Leather*, The World, East Village, New York, 1986

Traffic Violations Bureau in Hell's Kitchen, New York; DMC interior jail;
Run and Russell's father, Daniel Simmons, Sr., as The Warden (top right)

Penitentiary exterior shots, State Prison, Rahway, NJ, on the set of *Tougher Than Leather*, 1986

On the set of *Tougher Than Leather*,
restaurant scene at the Noho Star and performance
at The World, Lower East Side, New York, 1986

On the set of *Tougher Than Leather*, performance
at The World, Lower East Side, New York, 1986

On the set of *Tougher Than Leather*, Jay about to smash the bartender with his mug for making a rude comment, Lower East Side, New York, 1986

On the set of *Tougher Than Leather*, handing over Vic the hostage (Rick Rubin), Brooklyn Navy Yard, 1986

On the set of *Tougher Than Leather*, 1986

The World

Prospect Park

Bleecker Street

The World

When I first met the Beastie Boys my first thought was "these dudes are crazy."

Then I realized I was in love with MCA's rhyme style and that he wasn't just an amazing MC, but that Ad-Rock was just as ill. When I heard them all together finally with Mike D, and I saw them performing, I thought "these kids are cool." They had their own style. They were New York City personified. They just *smelled* like New York.

When we were touring together, I remember really well one of the first times I got to hang out with them. They had their own bus and we had our own bus. I was so happy to hang with them that I stayed on their bus one night 'til morning. I asked them stories about what they were doing in Manhattan—I'm from Queens—so it was crazy to hear how they operated in "The City" compared to what I was doing in my surroundings in Hollis. I wanted to hear all about it. They were telling me about Manhattan, teaching me stuff and telling me what all their crazy friends and crew were about. It was another world to me, off the chain, and I was just fascinated.

All I did was smoke weed back then, nothing more extreme. They had some other stuff they were doing, crazy white-boy shit, like Whip-Its, and all this stupid stuff. They were wild, and I thought I knew wild; but this was a whole other level of the game. I'll say now I didn't get into it that much, but I was just bugged out by their behavior, but it was fun as hell to be around them. I never really did figure out what a Whip-It was though.

As artists, the Beastie Boys were amazing. Between the three rappers— they even had DJ Double R, Rick Rubin, when I first met them— they were just ill, the illest, for real. They were taking beats that nobody else was taking and making pure hip-hop. "Hold It, Now Hit It" blew my mind. Then came "No Sleep 'Til Brooklyn" and that's the moment I realized they were on their way to becoming superstars. They were becoming something that other rappers—other than Run-DMC—weren't tapping into: mixing the rock and the rap together. With crazy hits like "(You Gotta) Fight for your Right (to Party!)"—it was taking them to the next level. Their artistry was truly through the roof for years to come.

It wasn't only the music that made them special; it was also what they wore, how they thought of themselves, and how they carried themselves in the rap game. They didn't get caught up in having to be people they weren't. If I were to think about the legacy of the Beastie Boys and what they would be known for, it's really just being cool. Like the New York Knicks, the New York Mets, and the five boroughs, the Beastie Boys are New York.

JOSEPH "REV RUN" SIMMONS

Live 1987

Together Forever tour, 1987

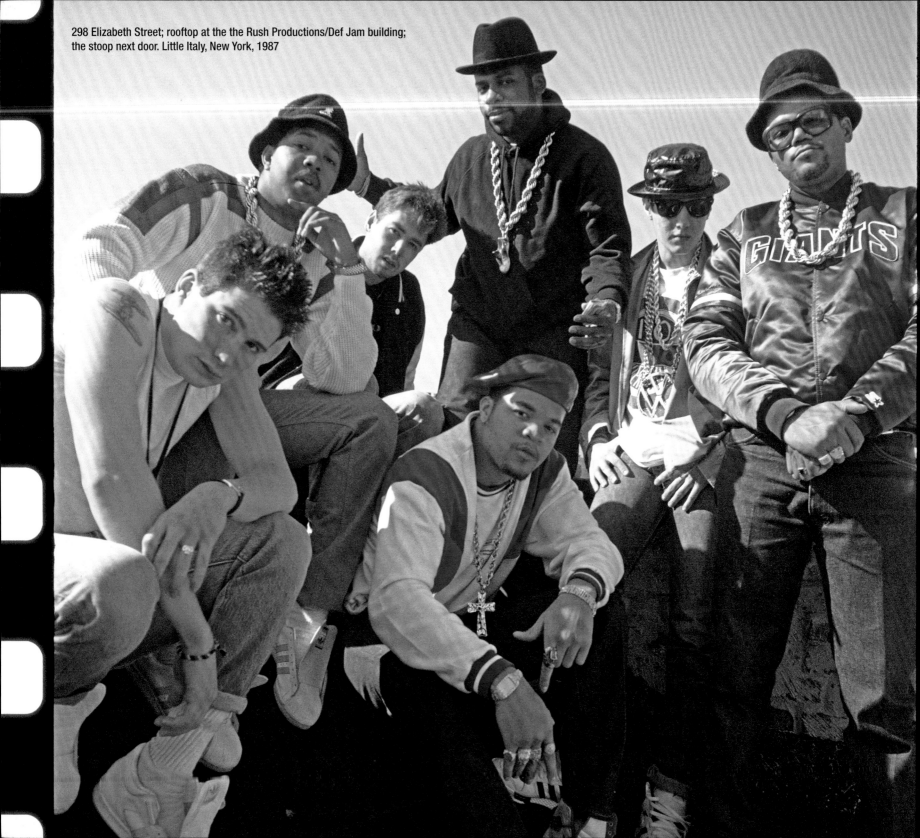

298 Elizabeth Street; rooftop at the the Rush Productions/Def Jam building; the stoop next door. Little Italy, New York, 1987

Capitol Theatre dressing room at the beginning of the *License To Ill* tour, Passaic, NJ, April, 1987

In back of "The Buildings" at 196 & Hollis, Queens, New York, 1985

Alley by "The Buildings" at 196 & Hollis, Queens, 1985

"The Buildings" at 196 & Hollis,
Queens, New York, 1985

162

The Ritz on East 11th Street, New York, 1985

Just after lunch at Angelica Kitchen,
2nd Ave. & 12th Street,
East Village, New York, mid-'90s

"Sucker MC's" changed the game; rap music changed our world.

When it came out it was a super-hot sticky New York City summer. It was the anthem. It played like every hour everywhere. When the temperature and humidity in NYC are blazing like that, windows have to be down in cars, stoops become living rooms, and "Sucker MC's" didn't play, it fucking blasted from every car and stoop and open apartment window and PA system plugged into a lamppost. This was raw, stripped down, real, b-boy rap music, revolutionary in the simplicity of its elements: a drum machine, some scratching, and relentless rhymes.

It was scary, exciting, and, for the time, way more punk than punk. In a crazy, bizarre, and surreal twisted bit of fate we would meet Run-DMC not too long after you heard that song everywhere. First, we met Run's brother and also manager, Russell Simmons, with Rick Rubin. Rick had produced a rap record by T La Rock & Jazzy Jay called "It's Yours," and Russell could not believe that anyone outside of his personal circle had made a record so loud and b-boy. They became fast friends and faster business partners, founding Def Jam together.

Through Russell, we were introduced to Run-DMC; we got to meet our heroes and we were not disappointed at all. We hung out with them and the Hollis crew in Queens, at clubs, at their shows, and in the studio.

We learned so fucking much from them, really, how to be a rap group: how to embrace differences in MC's voices and phrasing, how to play off of each other and how to come together and double or in our case triple up on a line or lines. Run-DMC were three very distinct very different personalities and they played into those strengths. Run was more manic, inspired, rapid-fire in his delivery. DMC was Rockin' Steady for real, he was the consistent vocal anchor, never straying too far in tone, pitch, cadence etc., even if conceptually his rhymes could go all over the place. Jam Master Jay (RIP) was the architect, the one who saw how it all would come together. He conceived their live shows—the lights, how DMC would come out, how Run would come out. He was the DJ and he put a great set together.

We were clueless when we got to be the first onstage opening act for their *Raising Hell* tour. We had a lot to learn about how to make a show, how not to just run around on stage shouting over each other, how to pace a show and ourselves. We didn't know shit, but we got to learn from the best.

The *Raising Hell* tour was rap finishing school and we had not only Run, D, and Jay but also Whodini, LL Cool J, and sometimes Doug E. Fresh as professors. Jay was also their style master, the bon vivant, the look creator for all their fashions. Fashion is really not the right word; it was heavier then that. Run-DMC were more then a group, they were icons. All black everything: The black Stetsons, the fresh-pressed black Lee jeans, the black Lee jackets or black leather bombers. The white-with-black stripes Adidas shell-toes with no laces, jail-style. It was a vibe, it set the tone, it set them apart from every rap group that came before them that was trying to look slick, like they had money to get dressed up to go out to a disco. Run-DMC wanted to let you know they were from the streets of Hollis, Queens, and it was authentic and undeniable. This was more than new music—this was a new language.

Getting to tour and work with these dudes was so sweet and such a gift. We got to peel back the curtain and be with the real people and not just the icons. Joe's (aka Run's) brain was always spinning, always running nonstop, his energy was manic. A million ideas a minute, "yo, you guys need to start a record like this—now here's a little story I got to tell . . . ." For real, he came running up to us on a Manhattan block yelling this over and over. D was a quiet genius, his mind wrapped up in his own internal brain's comic-book vision like the kid next to you in class scribbling in his notebook the whole time. Jay had a smile that would literally light up a room, he seemed confident because it felt like he could always see what was coming. That's why Jay's death was so fucking tragic and shocking. Not just because we lost an inspiration, loyal friend, and visionary, but because it truly put a sudden end to an amazing era during which Run-DMC reigned as rap's kings, setting the tone for all that was possible—or something that seemed impossible but was achievable—for Adam, Adam and me, and a whole world of aspiring rappers.

MICHAEL DIAMOND AKA MIKE D

Runyon Canyon,
Los Angeles, CA,
November 1991

Filming the video "Run's House" outside Madison Square Garden, 1988

UCLA Campus, 1987

175

Wonderland Elementary School; Adam's log cabin on Lookout Mountain Road, Laurel Canyon, Hollywood, CA, 1991

Times Square, New York, 1988

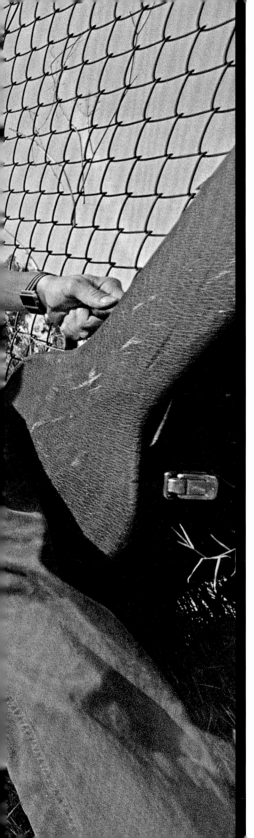

Near the Capitol Records Building, Franklin Ave. and 101 Freeway, Hollywood, CA, 1991

Hurricane onstage backing up Beastie Boys, and backstage with Bimmy on the *Raising Hell* tour.

The history that I share with Run-DMC and Jam Master Jay goes way back. We met in Hollis, Queens, on 205th Street at the local neighborhood park named 192. During the late '70s and '80s it was the stomping grounds for all the popular dudes to hang out. True to his craft, Joe (Run) was a cocky and confident MC. In his mind no one could rock the mic better then him. Basically, Joe knew how to command the crowd. Darryl (DMC) was the silent type off-stage; however, once he hit the stage he declared himself the "King of Rock" and his rhyming skills were a force to be reckoned with. Joe and D bounced off each other masterfully, and adding Jason (Jam Master Jay) was just the icing on the cake. Jason was the glue of Run-DMC; along with his exceptional skills as a DJ and his sense of style, Jay represented the essence of the Hollis flavor.

The *Raising Hell* tour was about to take off in 1986 when Jason came to my house and asked me to go on tour with him. He didn't want to leave me in the streets of Hollis—he knew my reputation for mischief. That tour showed me the world and kept me out of trouble. Run-DMC and Jam Master Jay were taking the world by storm. It was the beginning for kids and adults of all ethnicities dressing like Run-DMC and Jam Master Jay: they would all wear Adidas and black hats.

During the *Raising Hell* tour Beastie Boys were the opening act with only two songs. I initially met them at the Def Jam offices in the city. My first impression was that these are some wild and crazy white boys. They were New York–bred to the core and they dressed like they just woke up and threw on some clothes and then hit the stage. No coordination or thought put into the way they were going to perform. It was the opposite of what I was accustomed to. Consequently, in the middle of the tour, Dr. Dre from MTV quit DJing for them. With the Beasties stuck without a DJ, Jason suggested me because he knew I had turntable skills. The boys asked me to do it because the saw my skills firsthand when I practiced with Jason at the sound checks.

Adam Yauch (MCA) had a voice that sounded like he was hoarse. It was very unique and completely his own unmatched and undeniable sound that is recognizable all around the world. Adam Horovitz (Ad-Rock) had a crazy high-pitched voice that was also unique. Michael Diamond's (Mike D's) sound and energy was simply contagious on stage. I decided to DJ for the group. I figured this would keep me busy for some time, particularly because I didn't have any other job prospects at that moment. I saw this job as an opportunity to stay out of trouble. The Beasties were and still are super-talented individuals, and they had the ability to play instruments. However, my only pet peeve was that during performances they had food fights that were messy as fuck. I was too cool for that shit, so I insisted that when the shenanigans began they wouldn't get me or my attire messed up because I was not with the whip cream and beer all over my fresh gear—especially on my fresh sneakers. I've experienced many first-ever moments with the B-Boys: like I had never seen slam dancing prior to their shows. In my mind, they were the first to usher in slam dancing in hip-hop. They would do weird drugs like 'shrooms; I had never heard of that shit in my whole life.

The loss of MCA was a devastating blow in my life. I was at the DMV when I got that call from Ad-Rock. I grew up with them and love them like family. The loss of any loved one can be devastating on the soul; but losing people you consider brothers leaves crushing imprints on one's heart. It was a pleasure traveling with my good friends and being able to share a greatness that is recognized forever in the Rock & Roll Hall of Fame—it is truly humbling. From 1986 to 1997, they were the domineering groups of that era. The Run-DMC/Beastie Boys combination was a once-in-a-lifetime journey, and I was blessed to be a part of serving both.

WENDELL "DJ HURRICANE" FITE

Raising Hell tour, 1986

Onstage guests Whodini and LL Cool J

1986–1987

Mulholland Drive in the Hollywood Hills, Los Angeles, CA, 1991

On "the Ave.," Hollis, Queens, New York, 1988

On Long Island Rail Road tracks near Jamaica Park (aka Haggerty Park), Hollis, Queens, New York, 1988

Check Your Head era, tour warm-up show at the Avalon, Boston, MA, April 1992

Santa Monica, CA, 1991

Tibetan Freedom Concert #2,
Randall's Island, New York, June 1997

Chuck D wearing Jay's hat with Davy DMX, hanging with the crew, Elizabeth Street, New York, 1987

In 1983-84, sight and sound was everything; and "sound" totally

dominated the musical space. Video was about to become a factor and Run-DMC owned that starting line with "Rock Box" out the blocks. Although MTV claims they brought that video to the world, they kept the explosive possibilities of the hip-hop genre clamped down.

The Beasties to me, in entering the national and international planet of hip-hop and rap music, 1984–1988 especially, were like Jackie Robinson in reverse. The Glen E. Friedman capturing of the white punk B Boys was pioneering in itself. The style vocally was reminiscent of Kool Moe Dee Special K LA sunshine at the Treacherous 3 drop of a dime. The look was simulated gold chains, sneakers, jeans, shades—clothing easily found and associated with the haberdashery of "D Street," aka Delancey Street, in lower Manhattan. Or for that matter, found on "the Ave," aka Jamaica Avenue, in Queens, which supplied Run-DMC and Jam Master Jay. It totally was not easy for the Beasties back then because they were watched, scoped, and listened to every minute by the still small and grounded hip-hop world.

My experience with Run-DMC is something I can integrate into my career in hip-hop; in fact it's a primary reason for it. Radio station WBAU, where I worked, was a hip-hop center-point; it's also a stone's throw away from Hollis, Queens, about fifteen minutes across the border on Long Island. Bill Stephney connections made the new Rush Productions act a mainstay, and he did one of their first interviews. I was there at their first interview discussing their hot debut "It's Like That /Sucker MCs." I was there when they returned from their tours and claimed they got replenished coming to the station. They brought acts to the station with them. They previewed album tracks from *King of Rock* and *Raising Hell* months before they hit the public. We were a testing ground. Jam Master Jay promised me tickets at the 1985 FreshFest and walked up the ramp to give me those tickets. He invited us to the Madison Square Garden concert in 1986, where, point of fact, I met Glen E. for the first time. Jay was there when I handed my *Public Enemy Number 1* promo tape to Doctor Dre—then of group Original Concept, and later of *YO! MTV Raps* fame—and he asked for a copy. Of course Jay ushered us with his veteran mentorship cred. Humble as hell, yet firm as fuck, Jam Master Jay was the closest thing to a union leader hip-hop ever had, except for Eric B, maybe. His MCs Run and DMC were feral tigers on the mic. DMC was powerful and Run was just ridiculous with the fly flow attack. I traveled the world with them in 1988. I watched every show of Run-DMC and Jam Master Jay. Those memories mean the world to me. The photos—many of the best are here in this book—and the videos of that time are a visit to each emotional moment for what we now consider "history" in the greatest way.

Although the black rap group busted down the door, it couldn't get that US suburban nod of acceptance. And although the Beasties shattered the initial race curtain with an "official" rap record label and black management under Russell Simmons, they found they couldn't do it on studio and hype alone—gotta hit the stage and face the crowd.

I personally knew that the Beasties opening on the 1986 *Raising Hell* tour was gonna take them where no other white rap group had gone before. The arena-smashing reputation of Run-DMC was proven at the '84 and '85 Fresh Festivals sponsored by Swatch watches. That was fuel enough for the Beasties to bang their own tour in 1986–1987. The *License to Ill* album was the result of their push-backed CBS-distributed Def Jam epic debut. *License to Ill* detonated in suburban America with a bang, ricocheting off the usual cities and into the offbeat townships across North America and eventually abroad.

This is where Chuck D with Public Enemy come in. April 1, 1987: Public Enemy replaced CBS-label act Fishbone on *License To Ill*. No fools. We benefitted from the same machinery built by Def Jam: the promotions, the publicity of Bill Adler, and the solid base of management from Rush Productions. These things allowed us to grow our vision into a structure that was the antithesis of the Beasties. Finding that niche between the template of Run-DMC and Beastie Boys made it easier for us to achieve. We knew those b-boys from Queens and the white MCs from Brooklyn and Manhattan both had to get past the pioneer heat of the originals. They all had to be both impressive and inventive. We took their experience as education, and for preparation looking in as fans and curators.

Back to April 1987 from Erie to Allentown, PA, to Worcester, MA, I got a look at suburban America, that up-close dose of what we had all heard about. As Public Enemy, after we finished our opening act and passed the stage to rock outfit Murphy's Law, our members walked those arena floors to pass out promotional cards and flyers. We were up close and personal; not a lot of folks knew that we were those same menacing cats onstage earlier. We had seen their minds blown by just staring at us up there, and now we were watching these same fans reciting the lyrics to all these Beasties tracks.

The stage set-up was influential and worth copying. I personally drove the entire northeast, though occasionally Griff, Flav, and Terminator would take the wheel. I enjoyed driving to all these little towns my parents drove us to as kids. But this time I was performing there. As we got less nervous, the twenty-five-minute show started to find itself. Especially for me. I think the biggest threshold I personally hurdled was when Mike D was so beer-drunk at an Allentown show he fell out laughing in his verses—on the floor! I looked at DJ Hurricane (who coincidentally brought out his big boom box playing our record *Timebomb* on the nationally televised American Music Awards, before we even released a record, as the group b-boyed their way to the podium) and he shrugged his shoulders and smiled, like it was alright to even flub an entire verse as long as you entertained. That, believe it or not, was the moment I loosened up and went forward to Bring That Noise. I'm proof the Beasties are hip-hop tunnel blasters, indeed. And it's all captured in brilliant authenticity here by Glen E. Friedman.

CHUCK D - PUBLIC ENEMY

Brooklyn Bridge, 1990

Atwater Village, Los Angeles, CA, 1993

Lower East Side, New York, 1990

Hello Nasty listening party with friends, Greenwich Village, New York, 1998

BEASTIE BOYS

PHOTOGRAPHY © GLEN E. FRIEDMAN

First published in the United States of America in 2019 by
Rizzoli International Publications, Inc.
300 Park Avenue South, New York, NY 10010
www.rizzoliusa.com

© 2019 Glen E. Friedman / www.BurningFlags.com
Foreword: Chris Rock
Introduction: Glen E. Friedman
Texts: Chuck D, Michael Diamond aka Mike D, Wendell "DJ Hurricane" Fite, Adam Horovitz,
Darryl "DMC" McDaniels, Joseph "Rev Run" Simmons, Russell Simmons, Rick Rubin

Publisher: Charles Miers
Senior Editor: Jessica Fuller
Design: Mathieu Bitton
Production Manager: Colin Hough-Trapp
Managing Editor: Lynn Scrabis

2019 2020 2021 2022 2023 / 10 9 8 7 6 5 4 3 2 1

Printed in China

ISBN-13: 978-0-8478-6647-2
Library of Congress Catalog Control Number: 2019933619

Visit us online:
Facebook.com/RizzoliNewYork
Twitter: @Rizzoli_Books
Instagram.com/RizzoliBooks
Pinterest.com/RizzoliBooks
Youtube.com/user/RizzoliNY
Issuu.com/Rizzoli

Dedicated to the kids.